The
Moon
Gardener's
Almanac
2020

Created by Céleste
Edited by Thérèse Trédoulat
Translated by Mado Spiegler and Polly Lawson

First published in French as *Jardinez avec la Lune 2020*
by Éditions Rustica in 2019
This edition published in English by Floris Books in 2019
© 2019 Éditions Rustica, Paris
English version © 2019 Floris Books

British Library CIP data available
ISBN 978-178250-598-3
Printed and bound in Great Britain by Bell & Bain, Ltd

Floris Books supports sustainable forest management by
printing this book on materials made from wood that comes
from responsible sources and reclaimed material

MIX
Paper from
responsible sources
FSC® C007785

The
Moon
Gardener's
Almanac
2020

Floris
Books

Contents

Foreword

This almanac will help you to grow vegetables, fruit, flowers, shrubs and trees successfully and naturally from January 1 to December 31 using the lunar cycle as your guide. Based on 35 years' experience of gardening with the Moon, we explain how, by following the ascending or descending movements of the Moon and the constellations it crosses, you can optimise plant growth, leading to stronger, healthier plants, more abundant harvests, and crops rich in vitamins and flavour.

Day by day, the calendar suggests favourable times for working with different types of plant – leaf, flower, fruit or root – as well as highlighting less favourable times. Key gardening tasks and methods are described throughout the year, such as when and where to sow tomatoes or leeks, how to prune and graft fruit trees or roses, and when to plant a new hedge.

Our approach is completely natural and sustainable. We explain how you can respect the soil, use plant-based preparations instead of chemicals, and employ natural practices such as crop rotation and companion planting. All of these will make your garden more resilient and your crops healthier, avoiding pests and diseases.

Monthly charts encourage you to make notes about the weather, temperature and air pressure, which all influence our gardens. If our described tasks don't always suit your climate, our crop tables offer alternative favourable dates for sowing, planting, thinning, harvesting and pruning according to the Moon.

The United Nations has proclaimed 2020 the International Year of Plant Health, recognising the importance of plants in the sustainability of our world, as our main food resource, and for biodiversity. Gardening according to the cycles of the Moon can support and forward this goal.

We wish you happy reading and fruitful gardening throughout the year!

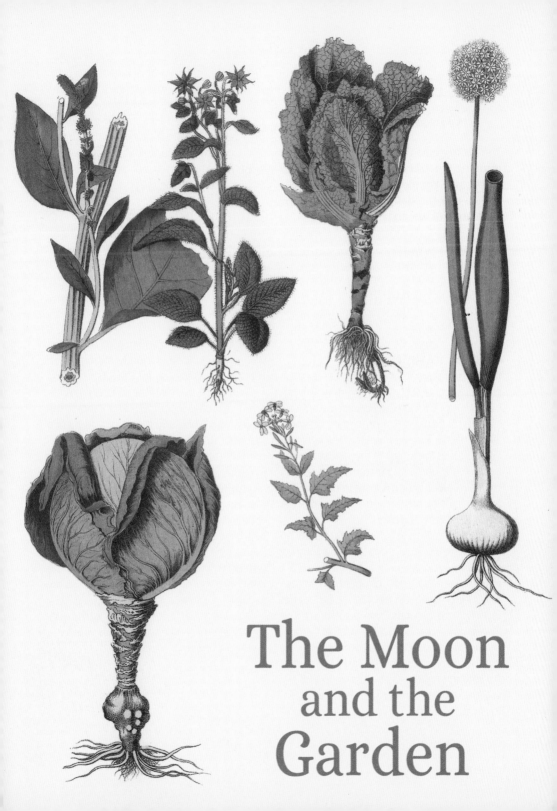

The Moon
and the
Garden

Rhythms
of the Earth

The life rhythms of our Earth involve three recurring processes: the annual cycle ruled by the Sun; the monthly cycle ruled by the Moon; and the daily cycle, ruled by the alternation of day and night.

Annual cycle
To help us understand the path of the Moon and its effects, which are the foundation of our gardening calendar, let's first look at the path of the Sun in the temperate zone of the Northern hemisphere.

Winter and spring
On the winter solstice, December 21 (the shortest day of the year, varying in the UK from 8 hours 3 minutes in Penzance, Cornwall, to only 5 hours 49 minutes in Lerwick, Shetland), the Sun rises well to the south-east and makes its lowest arc of the year, setting far in the south-west. By this time, many plants have died or are lying dormant in the soil. The Earth begins to prepare for its renewal – the new solar year is starting.

From the shortest day onwards to the summer solstice on June 20 (the longest day of the year, varying from 16 hours 23 minutes in Penzance to 18 hours 55 minutes in Lerwick), the Sun rises higher and higher in the sky. It ascends from Sagittarius, the lowest constellation, to Taurus and Gemini, the highest constellations. During these six months, very gradually, the Earth warms up. As the midday Sun gets higher in the sky and the days get longer, sap becomes active in the plant world.

It is then that we witness a veritable resurrection of nature, which guides the gardener's many tasks: pruning fruit and ornamental trees, soil preparation, sowing and replanting. In June, this time of intense growth comes to an end, as does summer sowing – harvesting is about to start.

Summer and autumn
On June 20, the day of the summer solstice, the Sun starts its descending arc. Its warm rays now have a drying effect. The days grow shorter, crops are harvested and the Earth starts to become bare. The rise of sap also slows down, causing tree leaves to dry out.

After the autumn equinox on September 22, gardeners can gradually start to work the soil in preparation for the following year.

With every harvest, the soil becomes less fertile, its vital resources exhausted by the crops, vegetables and fruit it has nourished. We need to help it restore itself by providing refined compost, enlivening manures and invigorating green manures.

During this period of deep inhalation, the Earth absorbs all the fertilising and rebalancing elements that gardeners provide. Sap descends into the roots again, leaves blow away, days get shorter and shorter and winter arrives. At the lowest point of the cycle, with the Sun back in Sagittarius, a new exhalation is about to begin.

Now, on warm, calm days, is the time for gardeners to plant perennials, trees and bare-root bushes.

Position of the Earth in relation to the constellations of the zodiac

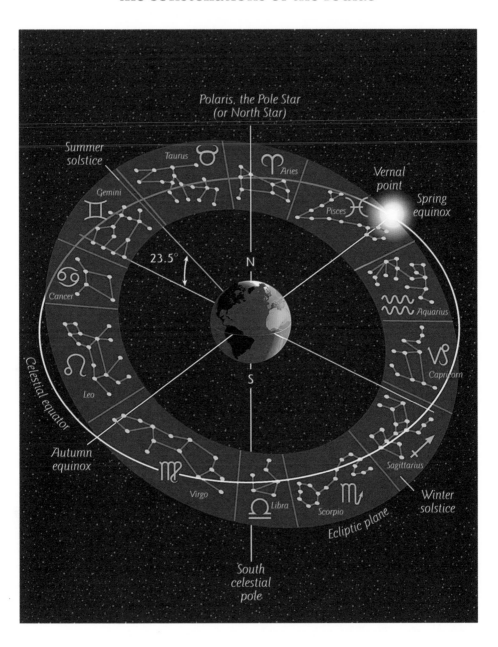

Polaris, the Pole Star (or North Star)

Summer solstice

Taurus

Aries

Gemini

Vernal point

Spring equinox

Pisces

23.5°

N

Cancer

Aquarius

Leo

Capricorn

S

Celestial equator

Autumn equinox

Virgo

Libra

Scorpio

Sagittarius

Winter solstice

Ecliptic plane

South celestial pole

Monthly cycle

The Moon takes one lunar month to orbit the Earth (approximately 27 days). Just as the Sun does in one year, in one month the Moon passes in front of every zodiacal constellation, with profound effects upon the Earth. The most spectacular example of this is illustrated by the phenomenon of the tides, which follow the rhythm of the 'Moon Day' of 24 hours and 50 minutes, of the Moon's rising, culminating, setting, reaching its lowest point and rising again. Scientific experiments have shown that the effect of the Moon can even be measured on inland water bodies.

Try looking up at the sky every evening. Whenever you can see the Moon, select landmarks (perhaps a tree, a house, or a hill) to locate it in relation to your environment. Day after day, you will observe the Moon ascending or descending in relation to these landmarks.

A number of online and print resources will give you daily times of the moonrise and moonset, which, on average, are about 50 minutes later every day.

Ascending moon: the lunar 'spring'

For 13½ days, the Moon ascends from Sagittarius, the lowest constellation, to Taurus/Gemini, the highest. It follows the path taken by the Sun from December 21 to June 20. During this time, sap rises in all plant life, swelling their aerial parts. Now is the time to remove grafts for later use (making sure to keep them at the right temperature until it's time to graft them). It is also time for sowing seeds, harvesting leafy vegetables, juicy fruit, and cutting flowers for bouquets.

Descending moon: the lunar 'autumn'

For the next 13½ days, as the Moon descends from Taurus to Sagittarius, it will appear lower and lower on the horizon every day. It follows the path taken by the Sun from June 20 to December 21. The sap goes back down into the roots and, as in October, the earth is at its most absorbent.

Using a tree as a landmark, look at the Moon and make a note of the time.
Look at it the next day, an hour later. If the Moon is higher, it is ascending; if it is lower, it is descending.

Now is the time to plant, replant, spread compost and organic manures, and prune. Plants recover better during this time: the roots reach deeper; the earth assimilates fertilizers well; hedges tolerate pruning without any problem, and the wounds left by removing tree branches heal better.

We call the ascending and descending movement of the Moon in a month (to be precise, 27 days, 7 hours, 43 minutes and 11 seconds) the sidereal period. **It is this ascending and descending motion that is relevant in the garden.**

Waxing and waning moon

Another cycle, called the synodic period (or synodic month) also takes approximately one month (to be precise, 29 days, 12 hours, 44 minutes and 3 seconds). **We do not take this cycle into account when gardening with the Moon.**

During the synodic month, the Moon waxes from New Moon to Full Moon, with the nearest side becoming increasingly visible. A thin sickle appears, which grows larger every day, to become the First Quarter and eventually the Full Moon.

The Moon then wanes to a New Moon. At the time of the Full Moon, it is fully illuminated by the Sun and looks completely round, waning daily until it disappears again at the time of the New Moon.

NOTE: Do not confuse the ascending moon with the waxing moon, or the descending moon with the waning moon.

Daily cycle

If you have ever camped in the woods, you will have been woken by a marvellous chorus of birdsong an hour or two before sunrise. The air grows colder, humidity rises, and plants also awaken, opening up to the morning dew and starting to swell with sap.

In the morning, when the dew has disappeared, it's time to sow seeds and pick lettuce, spinach, cucumbers and anything else that grows above ground.

Later, between midday and 3 pm, as the Sun starts to descend, the Earth turns back inward and forces move towards plants' roots. Now is the time to plant, replant, harvest root vegetables and finally, after sundown, to water.

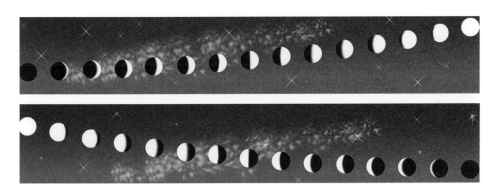

Top: The New Moon, invisible in the sky, waxes through crescent, First Quarter (half Moon), gibbous to Full Moon, getting bigger every day, until it appears as a full circle.

Bottom: The round Full Moon wanes through gibbous, Last Quarter (half Moon), crescent, and ends with the New Moon.

Tradition and the Moon

The Moon, being an ever-changing heavenly body, has always intrigued humans. We have long looked for connections between its phases and weather forecasts, health, births, animals and plants. For example, mushrooms can rarely be found at the time of the New Moon, even if the season and moisture are favourable, as this is their gestating period. They begin to appear on the fifth day of the lunar phase cycle and will be magnificently tender and succulent at the time of the Full Moon, or a little earlier. As the Moon wanes, their growth slows down and they gradually dry out.

Constellations of the Zodiac

Going back to prehistory, humans studied the stars. The first records come from the Chaldeans who could read the time of night in the sky, orient themselves and follow the seasons.

Lunar months or periods

There are four major lunar periods, each about a month in length.

Sidereal period

As we saw above, the sidereal period is the time it takes for the Moon to return to the same star in its revolution around the Earth. It is 27 days, 7 hours, 43 minutes and 12 seconds.

Synodic period

The synodic period refers to the phases of the Moon. As early as the third century BC, Babylonians had precisely calculated the average duration between two similar lunar phases (for example, two Full Moons) to an accuracy of 5 seconds. The average duration of the synodic period is 29 days, 12 hours, 44 minutes and 3 seconds.

Anomalistic (or apsidal) period

In its elliptical orbit the Moon is sometimes further from the Earth (apogee) and sometimes closer (perigee). The time from one perigee (or apogee) to the next is 27 days, 13 hours, 18 minutes and 33 seconds on average.

Draconitic (or nodal) revolution

The Moon's path through the stars does not exactly follow the Sun's path (the ecliptic). Its orbit is inclined by about 5 degrees to the ecliptic, crossing it twice at 'nodes'. The ascending node is where the Moon crosses from south of the ecliptic to north. The descending node is where it crosses from north of the ecliptic to south. The time between successive passages of the Moon through the same nodes is 27 days, 5 hours, 5 minutes and 36 seconds.

The twelve constellations

The 'fixed stars' have a constant relationship to each other even though they move across the sky, some rising and setting. Since ancient times these fixed stars have been seen in groups or constellations. The Sun, the Moon and the planets continually travel through a band of these fixed stars. This band consists of twelve constellations, which were seen as twelve animals or living beings in ancient Mesopotamia and Egypt. Hence the name *zodiac* (Greek *zoon*: animal, living being). You will always be able to pick out these constellations along the path followed by the Moon from the billions of stars surrounding us. The zodiac is a wide band of 18° around the line of the ecliptic, or ecliptic plane. Each star is a sun like ours. Some are much bigger than our Sun (Aldebaran, the most brilliant star in Taurus, has a diameter 36 times that of the Sun). Each of these stars, like our Sun, sends us its distant rays and we benefit from the influences of the constellation and its sky region. Let's take a look at these possible influences.

The precession of the equinoxes

Between March 20 and 22, depending on the year, the Sun crosses the celestial equator at the *vernal point*, marking the beginning of spring. This very specific point does not stay fixed in relation to the stars. It moves back every year by a 50 seconds of arc which comes to 1° over 72 years, or 30° over 2,160 years. This means that the vernal point which in Greek times was in the constellation of Aries, has now moved to the constellation of Pisces.

The Greeks divided the zodiac into twelve equal *signs* of 30° each. These *signs* are still used in astrology today. However for this calendar it is the visible *constellations* which are used. Because of the precession of the equinox the signs and constellations have shifted on average by one constellation.

The four elements

Just as a plant is composed of four parts – root, leaf, flower and fruit – the twelve zodiacal regions each have affinities with one of the main elements of the universe – earth, water, air and fire. These form four types of impulse regularly distributed around the Earth, and each impulse has a specific effect on particular parts of plants.

When it passes in front of a constellation, the Moon activates these different forces. It captures them, adds its own power then reflects them back to Earth just as it reflects the light of the Sun. Whenever gardeners work the soil, they make it more receptive to the influence of these elements.

The earth element

Attuned to the constellations of **Taurus, Virgo and Capricorn**, the earth element affects the buried part of the plant: the root. When the Moon passes in front of these earth constellations, it's the optimum time to enrich and prepare the soil, plant seeds, thin, weed, and transplant the seedlings of root vegetables. In particular, these constellations influence root and bulb crops such as garlic, onions, carrots, turnips, potatoes and radishes. When we respect this timing, these vegetables are more resistant to parasites

Constellations of the zodiac

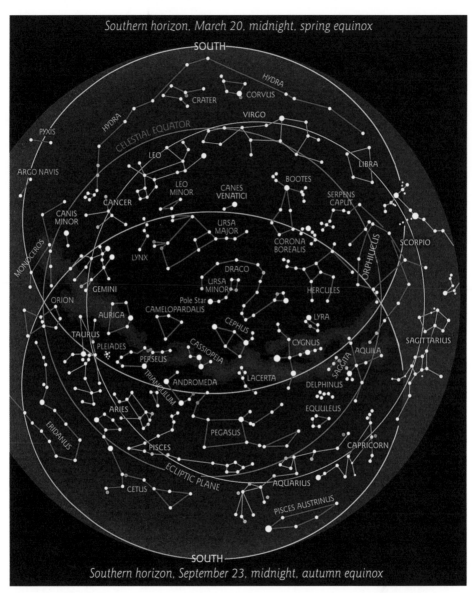

The top circular area of the illustration represents the sky at midnight on March 20, day of the spring equinox; the lower circular area, the sky at midnight on September 23, day of the autumn equinox. The constellations of the zodiac are along the ecliptic, the path followed every year by the Sun, and every month by the Moon.

when harvested, and their nutritional value, taste and productivity increase.

The water element

Active in **Cancer, Scorpio and Pisces**, the water element particularly influences moisture-loving parts of the plant: the stem and leaves.

Gardeners should use times when the Moon passes in front of water constellations to care for leaf and stem crops such as lettuce, spinach and asparagus. Doing so will yield beautiful, tender, crunchy leaves and delicate, tasty asparagus.

The air element

Due to its affinity with **Gemini, Libra and Aquarius**, the air element expresses itself in the fragrance of flowers, plants and vegetables. For optimum results, gardeners should use times when the Moon passes in front of air constellations to take care of flowers and flower crops such as artichokes, cauliflowers and broccoli.

Variable durations

The zodiac constellations are different lengths, which results in unequal time periods for gardening certain types of plant. In practice, this means that gardeners will always have more time for root vegetables than for flowers.
Earth constellations occupy:
Capricorn 28° + Taurus 36° + Virgo 46° = 110°
Water constellations: Pisces 38° + Cancer 21° + Scorpio 31° = 90°
Fire constellations: Sagittarius 30° + Aries 24° + Leo 35° = 89°
Air constellations: Aquarius 25° + Gemini 28° + Libra 18° = 71°

The fire element

Related to **Aries, Leo and Sagittarius**, the fire element brings the warmth needed to ripen fruit and the seeds necessary for reproduction. Gardeners should use times when the Moon is in fire constellations to care for fruit and seed crops such as apricots, apples, peas, tomatoes and beans.

When gardening by element, be aware that some constellations are isolated, e.g. Gemini and Cancer, while others almost overlap, e.g. Taurus and Aries.

NOTE: The calendar gives very precise timings for the transition between ascending and descending moons (or vice versa), as well as for the passage between constellations. Gardeners should not rush to work as soon as it is 'the right time', for the effect is not instantaneous. Instead take time to think and plan the garden long-term. Also, remember that schedules are given for Greenwich Mean Time, so if you are not in Britain or Ireland you will need to make adjustments for local times (see p. 37).

What if I can't always follow the Moon faithfully?

It's not always possible to strictly follow the Moon; it might be too cold, or just impossible to make time to garden. You can compensate by making sure you perform as many pre-harvest tasks at the most favourable time. If possible, prioritise the preparation and enrichment of soil, sowing and planting.

Current position of the zodiac constellations
and corresponding symbols in Western astrology

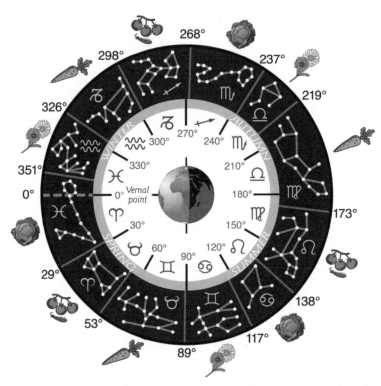

The inner circle shows the twelve signs of the zodiac as shown in horoscopes. In astrology, their size is a constant (30° each). The outer circle shows the constellations as they should be observed in gardening: for instance, the smallest constellation, Libra, covers 237°– 219° = 18°, not 30° as in astrology. **When you garden, make sure you follow the actual duration of each constellation as our calendar does.**

Zodiac constellations	♈ Aries	♌ Leo	♐ Sagittarius
	♉ Taurus	♍ Virgo	♑ Capricorn
	♊ Gemini	♎ Libra	♒ Aquarius
	♋ Cancer	♏ Scorpio	♓ Pisces

Explanation of gardening symbols

LEAF
Water constellations

FLOWER
Air constellations

ROOT
Earth constellations

SEED & FRUIT
Fire constellations

Lunar Irregularities

There are times when the Moon does not provide the optimum conditions for gardening, specifically during periods of significant lunar change. Be sure to wait 5 hours either side of a moon node, apogee or perigee before gardening and, if possible, wait even longer if there is an eclipse.

Perigee and apogee

The Moon travels on an elliptical orbit, in which the centre of Earth is one of the foci. Every lunar month, the Moon passes through the **perigee**, the point where its distance from the Earth is smallest (356,500 km/221,500 miles) and its speed greatest (moving 15° per day). Conversely, at the **apogee**, the Moon is at its most distant point (406,700 km /252,700 miles) and its speed is at its slowest (moving 12° per day). Gardening during the Moon's perigee can result in weak and sickly plants, while vegetation can be shrunken, constricted and prone to sickness when planted during the apogee.

If the Full Moon or the New Moon coincide with the perigee, there is an even greater likelihood of irregularities, particularly if it coincides with an equinox or solstice. This was the case during Storm Martin, which violently swept across Europe in December 1999. Likewise, the devastating tsunami of December 2004 took place at the time of the winter solstice, on the eve of the Moon's apogee on December 27.

To avoid a weak harvest, watch out for these situations: Sun at the time of equinox or solstice + Full Moon, and New Moon at the perigee.

Moon nodes

The plane of the Moon's orbit is at an angle of 5.1° from the plane of the ecliptic, along which the Sun travels. The Moon crosses this plane twice every month, at two points called nodes. (The ascending node is when the Moon crosses from south of the ecliptic to north. The descending node is where it crosses from north of the ecliptic to south.) When the Full Moon or New Moon coincides with a node, there is an eclipse of the Moon or the Sun. Plants are particularly sensitive at these times, so keep in mind that sowing will produce sterile seeds. You may also often notice that the sky is white during a moon node. Again, it is best not to garden 5 hours before or after this point.

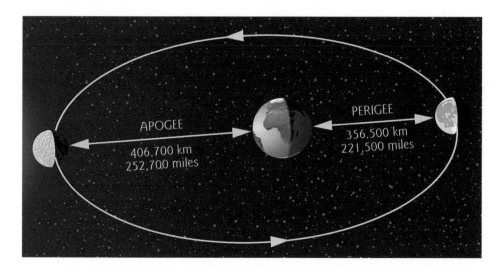

APOGEE
406,700 km
252,700 miles

PERIGEE
356,500 km
221,500 miles

The Moon after Easter

While the true power of the Moon is constantly being discussed and argued, in agriculture the influence of the Moon after Easter has always been unquestioned. The most ancient texts bear witness to it, and gardeners still watch out for its coming.

Easter always occurs after the Full Moon after the spring equinox. At this time of year, the Sun is already high and the days last longer. When the sky is clear, daytime temperatures begin to rise, allowing small seedlings and budding fruit to soak up the warmth. After sunset, the cold returns and the thermometer dips; gradually a cold dew covers the plants and it can sometimes still be frosty at dawn. Young plants can often suffer during these cold nights, so keep any weather protection in place during this time.

Eclipses

If the New Moon occurs near a node (see p. 19) there is a solar eclipse. If the Full Moon coincides with a node, there will be a lunar eclipse. Plants are extremely sensitive to these phenomena, so it is advisable to avoid gardening during these times.

Moon nodes

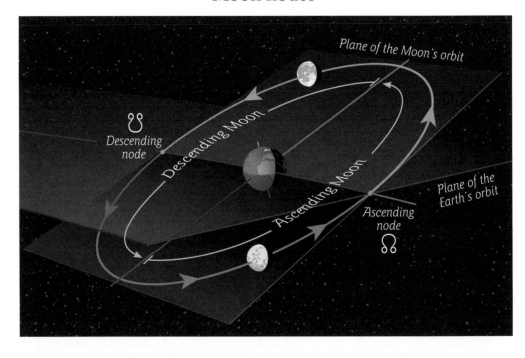

The Moon and Plants

Every type of plant is affected differently by the Moon's position in each constellation. Vegetables can be classified as root, leaf, flower or fruit depending on the plant part we consume. For example, beetroot, onion and potatoes are all roots; chard, cabbage and Brussels sprouts are leaves; artichokes and broccoli are flowers; and tomatoes, aubergine (or eggplant) and peas are fruit, as are grains and fruit trees.

Root, leaf, flower or fruit?

Below is a partial list of vegetables, ornamental plants and fruit trees.
Adapt the list to match what you plan to cultivate.

Root	Leaf	Flower	Seed and Fruit
Beet(root)	Asparagus	Broccoli	Aubergine (eggplant)
Carrot	Brussels sprout	Cauliflower	Berries
Celeriac	Cabbage	Globe artichoke	Broad bean (fava)
Chervil (root)	Cardoon		Chilli pepper
Chicory*	Celery	Flowering bushes	Courgette (zucchini)
Chinese artichoke	Chicory*	– Forsythia	Cucumber
Garlic	Cress	– Lilac	Fruit trees
Horseradish	Dandelion	– Magnolia	Green bean
Jerusalem artichoke	Endive*	– Rose	Lentils
Leek	Fennel	– Wisteria	Marrow
Onion	Grass		Melon
Parsnip	Herbs	Flowers	Peas
Potato	Lettuce	– Annuals	Pepper
Radish	Lamb's lettuce	– Biennials	Pumpkin
Salsify	(mâche)	– Bulbs	Strawberry
Shallot	Ornamental bushes	– Perennials	Squash
Swede (rutabaga)	Purslane		Tomato
Turnip	Rhubarb		Watermelon
	Rocket (arugula)		
	Romaine lettuce		Grains
	Sorrel		– Barley
	Spinach		– Corn
	Swiss chard		– Oats
			– Rye
			– Wheat

*NOTE: *The cultivation of endive and chicory has two stages. The aim with the original seeding is to produce strong roots, so sow the seed in an ascending moon, on a root day. Pull them up, again on a root day, and let them dry a few days on the ground. The second stage – forcing – aims to produce beautiful leaves, ideal for cooking or salads. This is achieved by replanting the roots and harvesting the leaves on leaf days.*

Gardening According to the Moon's Position

In order to benefit from the influence of the Moon, particular types of plants should be sown according to whether the Moon is ascending or descending, and which constellation it is passing through. For example, by looking at the grid below we can see that lettuce (a leaf crop) is best sown in an ascending moon when the Moon is in Pisces, and that forsythia (a flower) should be planted in a descending moon when the Moon passes in front of Gemini or Libra.

Movement of the Moon	Constellation/ element	Type of plant	Task
Ascending	Sagittarius ♐ Fire 30°	Seed and fruit	In the ascending Moon:
Ascending	Capricorn ♑ Earth 28°	Root	• Sow
Ascending	Aquarius ♒ Air 25°	Flower	• Harvest leaf crops (spinach, lettuce)
Ascending	Pisces ♓ Water 38°	Leaf	• Harvest flower crops (artichokes)
Ascending	Aries ♈ Fire 24°	Seed and fruit	• Harvest fruit (tomatoes, peas, apples)
Ascending	Taurus ♉ Earth 36°	Root	• Take cuttings and graft
Ascending	Gemini ♊ Air 28°	Flower	

Movement of the Moon	Constellation/ element	Type of plant		Task
Descending	Gemini ♊ Air 28°	Flower		In the descending Moon:
Descending	Cancer ♋ Water 21°	Leaf		• Propagate from cuttings
Descending	Leo ♌ Fire 35°	Seed and fruit		• Enrich the soil • Thin seedlings • Transplant seedlings
Descending	Virgo ♍ Earth 46°	Root		• Harvest root crops (carrots, turnips)
Descending	Libra ♎ Air 18°	Flower		• Prune and cut back
Descending	Scorpio ♏ Water 31°	Leaf		• Divide plants • Layer
Descending	Sagittarius ♐ Fire 30°	Seed and fruit		

The descending Moon ends in Gemini and the ascending Moon starts in Sagittarius. Following our calendar allows you to match your garden activities with the movement of the Moon in the sky.

Plants in their Environment

As a living being fixed in the soil, a plant is entirely dependent on its environment. On one hand, it raises its stem towards the sky to catch the light and warmth of the Sun, while on the other, it plunges its roots into the Earth looking for everything it needs to grow and reproduce. Food, water, minerals and cosmic life forces are all essential to a plant's survival, and the condition of the soil is vitally important in ensuring these resources are successfully delivered.

Cosmic forces

We can aid plants' sensitivity to cosmic influences by doing all we can to increase their receptiveness. Suppressing artificial obstacles to cosmic forces, making the atmosphere permeable, and introducing easily assimilated food into the soil all help to optimise plants' sensitivity. By making the helpful cosmic forces as accessible as possible, we will see the benefit in the roots, leaves, flowers and fragrances of our gardens.

Most cosmic forces, in particular those of the Moon, act only indirectly on plants; before roots can take them in, they are absorbed by the soil – depending on its receptivity and the current position in the lunar cycle. The health and vigour of our vegetables call for well-balanced, aerated and receptive soil.

Soil

In order to develop properly, plants need air, light and soil in which to take root and absorb water and nutrients. These elements are more easily available to plants when the soil's fertility has been restored with beneficial manures and enrichments, which are active during the most favourable lunar dates.

Every soil is different; whether sandy, clay or lime, it will need to be loosened regularly and be fertilised with appropriate growth aids and enlivening manures. **Ensure chemical fertilisers are not used:** besides their harmful effect on crops, they make the soil impervious to the influence of cosmic forces. When gardening with the Moon, feed soil exclusively with well-ripened compost, animal manure, green manures and liquid slurries of vitalising plants, for example nettles and comfrey. Soil should not remain bare between two crops: depending on the season, sow clover, rye, vetch or mustard to contribute helpful organic matter and protect the soil from weathering (see 'Growing green manures' and 'Mulching' p. 26–27).

Air and light

Sunlight is integral to a plant's development. Gardeners should make sure that their growing space has the maximum amount of light, but shouldn't hesitate to plant a hedge of mixed bushes on the side of the prevailing wind for protection. The hedge will filter the air, protecting plants from chemical treatments which might have been applied in neighbouring properties, and will also shelter birds that feed on aphids, caterpillars and unwanted insects.

Improving and feeding the soil

Gardeners who use the Moon can also make the most of their soil by following the general principles of biodynamic gardening (see Further Reading, p. 119). Work the soil without disrupting the direction of the top layer, and improve it with natural matter that will be organically assimilated by the plants on decomposing. Year on year, this will gradually improve the fertility of the soil, enabling the successful growth of healthy vegetables, flowers and fruit.

Working the soil

Soil is alive. It contains millions of micro-organisms invisible to the eye, as well as being home to bigger inhabitants such as earthworms and beetles. On the soil's surface, we find aerobic micro-organisms that need oxygen to survive, while anaerobic organisms live deeper down. Whenever the soil is ploughed, by hand or machine, the top layers are inverted, together with the micro-organisms they contain, which subsequently often die. Yet these minuscule creatures and bacteria are a gardener's allies. They break down organic matter, transforming it into humus, which plants can then use for food and growth.

With this in mind, it is vital that we adopt 'soft' practices for aerating the soil, without disturbing it. Adapted hand cultivators should be used where possible (consisting of two handles connected by a bar at the bottom, in which three to five vertical tines are inserted) and soil should be worked while walking backwards. Plunging the tines into the soil and lowering the handles produces a crumbly, aerated soil, which will in turn create a loose, aerated growing surface.

Making compost

Waste from the garden and kitchen can be turned into excellent compost. Dry or brown garden waste, including bush cuttings (crushed first, if possible) and dead leaves, and green and wet waste from lawn mowing, weeds and vegetable peelings can all be used to create homemade compost. Plants that have gone to seed, sick plants or vegetation affected by parasites (whether eggs, larvae or fully formed) should be avoided, in addition to rose cuttings, fruit-tree leaves and wormy fruit. Waste should be piled up in a corner of the garden or in a composter, alternating dry and wet matter in layers approximately 25 cm (10 in) thick. Ideally, the waste should touch the ground to allow earthworms to rise into the pile and break everything down. You can speed up the process by adding earth worms, which will digest your waste. If necessary, water the pile once a month to hasten the process further, and make sure you cover the pile to keep it warm, which will speed up fermentation. Your compost will be ripe in approximately 10 months. Use it at the end of winter, incorporating it superficially into the soil, spreading it between flowers, in the planting holes of 'greedy' vegetables, fruit trees or berry bushes, and in the mixture you use to repot any potted plants.

Introducing natural fertilisers

More and more garden centres sell 'natural fertilisers' containing the same elements as chemical fertilisers: nitrogen (N), phosphorus (P) and potassium (K). The nitrogen often comes from feather meal, horns and castor-oil cake, while phosphorus is provided by fish bones, natural phosphate and beet stillage. They decompose slowly and are absorbed gradually, feeding the soil, renewing its fertility and gently nourishing the plants without harming them. However, natural fertilisers must be introduced ahead of growing time, either in autumn or late winter when the soil is being prepared. Recommended dosages will be indicated on the product package and should be adhered to. More specific fertilisers can be added later in the growing cycle for demanding crops, but dried blood and guano should be avoided: their rapid action is similar to that of chemical fertilisers and they have a tendency to leach out when it rains.

Growing green manures

Green manures are sown specifically to improve the structure of the soil; to enrich and cover it so that it won't get packed when it rains, in addition to fighting some parasites and weeds. When choosing green manure crops, consider the duration of their growth cycle, their uses and the nature of your soil. Green manures find their place between the harvest of one crop and the seeding or planting of another in the same patch, if there is a long gap, for instance between spring spinach and autumn turnips. You can also use them in late summer and autumn in a bed you plan to keep fallow until next spring. In the latter case, the crop will have

to be frost hardy. Green manures not killed by frost should be cut back after they bloom to make sure they don't reseed themselves, then crushed and buried. Do not plant a green manure crop of the same family as the vegetable that precedes or follows it (see table and 'Crop Rotation' p. 28).

Sweet lupin is sown from March to July (1–2 kg/100 m², 2–4 lb/100 sq yd). The white lupin prefers heavy soils, while the yellow lupin likes poor, sandy soil.

White mustard is sown from March to August (150–200 g/100 m², 4–6 oz/100 sq yd) but should not be grown immediately before or after cabbages, turnips or radishes. It is good for heavy, even limey soil and grows quickly, fighting nematodes and weeds.

Phacelia can be sown from March to August (150–200 g/100 m², 4–6 oz/100 sq yd) and should be buried two months later. Phacelia grows very quickly, fights nematodes and its flowers attract numerous pollinators. There are no vegetables in this plant family so it can be grown between any variety.

Buckwheat should be sown from May to August (500–600 g/100 m², 14–18 oz/100 sq yd) as this crop is not frost hardy. It is especially useful when used in poor acid soils to loosen soil and choke weeds.

Rye can be sown in September or October (2 kg/100 m², 4 lb/100 sq yd). Completely hardy, it should be buried in spring. Suited to poor soils on the acidic side and for fighting weeds, rye can also be grown together with vetch (500 g/1lb rye and 700 g/1½ lb vetch per 100 m² /100 sq yd). The latter's tendrils hang on to its stems, and this combination has been found to improve nitrogen content in the soil.

White clover is sown from April to September (50–100 g/100 m², 1½–3 oz/ 100 sq yd) in cold heavy soils. Dig it under in autumn and spring, and remember that this perennial can also be grown in paths.

Mulching

Another way to keep soil covered between crops is to spread mulch over empty beds. This keeps the soil cool between rainfall or watering, and slows the growth of weeds, making them easier to pull. Some mulches can also enrich or lighten soil, but **wait until the earth warms up in spring before adding them, preferably in May.**

Prepare the soil by weeding carefully and watering, before spreading a 5 cm (2 in) layer of mulch on top, which can include grass mowings, hemp or linen chaff, cocoa shells or crushed straw. The layer should be renewed regularly, as grass mowings break down particularly fast. Spread the mulch at the end of spring, and turn it in autumn.

Choosing plants and their location

Over the years, gardeners have come to notice that some plants help each other out – they are 'companions'– whereas others seem to 'dislike' each other. These affinities can be used when planning your garden, and if successfully paired, your vegetables and other plants will be stronger as a result and more resistant to parasites and disease. Taking the time to establish yearly rotations and companion plants can also help avoid the need for chemical treatments. This process becomes easier as time passes, and you will be well rewarded. Remember that some vegetables need to be pollinated, so sow them next to plants that attract honeybees.

Attracting pollinators

Bees and other pollinating insects are becoming rarer, despite their usefulness. To encourage their presence in your garden, sow or plant borage, cosmos flowers, marigolds, phacelia or calendula along garden paths and between vegetable rows. Choose simple flowers, which make foraging easier, and when planting herbs, plant more of them than you need so you can allow some to bloom. Pollinators love chives, rosemary, savoury and thyme, and as they visit them, they will also visit vegetable flowers nearby – aubergine (eggplant), cucumber, squash, strawberries, beans, peas and tomatoes – making for a more abundant harvest.

Choosing companion plants

Although it is not entirely clear how, some plants seem to encourage their neighbours' growth. This is certainly the case with borage, nasturtium, marigold, sage and sunflowers. These plants also attract pollinating insects and repel parasites, so plant them throughout your garden (see table on p. 29).

Crop rotation

The term 'crop rotation' refers to the succession of crops on the same plot of garden. It is determined by plants' own cycles, rather than by the calendar year. Here's an example of how to implement crop rotation in a vegetable garden:

Year 1: divide your vegetable garden into four squares of the same surface area. **In square 1** sow legumes such as peas and beans that contribute nitrogen to the soil. After the harvest, cut the stems so that they decompose in the ground. **In square 2** plant leaf vegetables such as cabbage, lettuce and spinach. In **square 3** plant roots: potatoes, beets, turnips and so on. **Divide square 4 in two:** keep one half fertiliser-free for undemanding plants such as bulbs (garlic, shallot, onion); in the other half, incorporate compost and plant or sow vegetables that need a rich soil, for example aubergine (eggplant), cucumber, squash, melons, tomatoes and flower crop (broccoli, cauliflower etc.).

In the following years, rotate the vegetables in the squares:
Year 2: In square 1 leaf vegetables replace legumes, benefiting from the nitrogen left behind. **In square 2** root vegetables follow leaves, looking for food deeper in the soil. **Square 3** will be divided: one half for demanding, the other half for undemanding vegetables. Cultivate legumes in **square 4**.
In years 3 and 4, keep shifting crops around the squares, always in the same order. **In year 5** cultivate the same vegetables in the same squares as in year 1.

Some plants remain in place for several seasons (perennial herbs, artichokes, asparagus, strawberries, small fruit, rhubarb etc.) on the edges of the garden and along paths. Place them a little to the north and west depending on their sun requirements, so that they won't overshadow the crops.

A few location rules

In summary, following these simple rules will help prevent deficiencies and disease:

- **Respect individual plants' preferences** regarding soil fertility (some plants are greedy, others less demanding or downright abstemious) and the acid or alkaline nature of the soil.
- **Consider 'companion planting'** – favourable or unfavourable proximities (see table on p. 29).
- **Practise crop rotation** – avoid cultivating plants of the same family in the same location two years in a row (see table below).

Green manure plants

Plant family	Herbs, grains, vegetables	Green manures
Apiaceae	carrot, celery, chervil, fennel, parsnip, parsley	
Asteraceae	artichoke, cardoon, chicory, tarragon, lettuce, salsify	
Brassica	cabbage, cress, white turnip, radish, horseradish, rocket	rape, white mustard, brassica
Chenopodiaceae	beets, spinach, Swiss chard	
Cucurbitaceae	cucumber, squash, melon, watermelon, pumpkin	
Fabaceae	beans, lentils, peas	lupin, alfalfa, sainfoin, clover, vetch

Plant family	Herbs, grains, vegetables	Green manures
Hydrophyllaceae		phacelia
Lamiaceae	basil, Chinese artichoke, mint, oregano, rosemary, sage, thyme	
Liliaceae	garlic, asparagus, chive, shallot, onion, leek	
Poaceae	oats, wheat, corn, barley, rye	oat, rye
Polygonaceae	sorrel, rhubarb	buckwheat
Solanaceae	aubergine (eggplant), pepper, potato, tomato	

Companion planting

As discussed, plants influence each other when grown together; some encourage growth, while others dislike being in close proximity. It is well known that leeks keep away the carrot fly, the proximity of carrots discourages leek moths, and radishes are sweeter when grown near lettuce. The table below will help you to discover other associations and which crops to separate.

✓ : friends
✗ : enemies

	asparagus	aubergine (eggplant)	beet(root)	broad bean (fava)	cabbage	carrot	celery	cucumber	garlic	green bean	leek	lettuce	melon	onion	pea	potato	squash/pumpkin	radish	shallot	spinach	marrow/courgette	strawberry	tomato	turnip
asparagus								✓	✓	✓	✓	✓			✓								✓	
aubergine (eggplant)								✓									✓	✓						
beet(root)				✓	✗	✓		✓	✓	✗	✓			✓		✗		✓	✓	✓			✗	
broad bean (fava)			✓		✓	✓	✓	✓	✗	✓	✗	✓		✗	✗	✓		✓	✗	✓	✓			
cabbage			✓	✓		✓	✓	✓		✓		✓		✗	✓	✓		✗	✗	✓		✗		
carrot			✗	✓	✓		✓		✓	✓	✓	✓		✓	✓	✗		✓	✓	✓			✓	
celery			✓	✓	✓	✓		✓		✓	✓	✗		✓	✗								✓	
cucumber	✓			✓	✓		✓			✓			✗	✓	✓	✗							✗	
garlic	✓		✓	✗		✓				✗	✗	✓		✗	✓							✓	✓	
green bean	✓	✓	✓	✓	✓	✓	✓	✓	✗		✗	✓	✓	✗	✗	✓		✓	✗	✓	✓	✓		✓
leek	✓		✗	✗		✓	✓		✗			✓		✓	✗	✗			✓				✓	✓
lettuce	✓		✓	✓	✓	✓	✗	✓	✓	✓	✓		✓	✓	✓			✓	✓	✓	✓	✓		✓
melon						✗		✓	✓					✓	✗						✓	✗		
onion			✓	✗	✗	✓		✓		✗	✓	✓		✗	✗			✓			✓	✓	✓	✗
pea	✓			✗	✓	✓	✓	✗	✗	✗	✓	✓	✗			✓		✓	✓	✓			✗	✓
potato			✗	✓	✓	✗	✗	✗	✓	✓		✗	✗	✗	✓		✗			✗			✗	
squash/pumpkin		✓														✗		✓					✓	
radish		✓	✓	✓	✗	✓	✓		✓		✓			✓					✓	✗			✓	
shallot			✓	✗	✗	✓				✗		✓		✓	✗	✓						✓	✓	
spinach			✓	✓	✓	✓			✓	✓	✓	✓		✓				✓				✓	✓	✓
marrow/courgette			✓						✓	✓	✗	✓		✗				✗					✗	
strawberry				✗			✓	✓	✓	✓		✓						✓	✓				✓	
tomato	✓	✗			✓	✓	✗	✓		✓		✓		✓	✗	✗	✓	✓	✓	✓	✓	✗		✓
turnip						✓		✓		✓				✗	✓			✓		✓			✓	

Fighting disease and parasites

Don't reach for the spray pump the minute you spot aphids or powdery mildew. Take preventive action by encouraging the development of helpful insects, introducing companion plants whose fragrance repels parasites, or using plant-based preparations. Pesticides should only be used as a last resort.

Encouraging helpful insects

Learn to recognise not only adult insects but also their eggs and larvae, so as not to destroy them mistakenly. Ladybirds, hoverflies and lacewings are your allies and will devour aphids. If you plant nectar-rich flowers and provide natural or manmade shelters where they can spend the winter, these helpful creatures will be ready for action as soon as the first pests appear in spring. Most importantly, use chemical treatments as little as possible. If aphids appear before their predators, cut back the affected parts of the plant, giving the helpful insects time to develop ahead of the next generation of pests.

Making plant preparations

Herbal preparations are made by macerating certain plants before they go to seed and spraying the resulting 'tea' to fight disease or parasites. Always use rainwater and wooden containers (never metal), preferably closed, to mix preparations. Since these liquids do not keep very long, be ready to prepare several batches in the course of a growing season.

Two techniques are used: manures (or macerations) and teas (or decoctions). **For manures**, soak the plants in cold water until all soluble substances are dissolved, then filter and dilute the manure before use. You can use ferns to fight aphids and slugs; nettles against aphids and various diseases; and elder to fight flea beetles, aphids and thrips, and to prevent as well as fight cabbage white butterflies and leek moths. **For teas**, soak plants for an entire day, then boil over a low heat for 20 minutes, allow to cool, then filter for use. Horsetail is good for all diseases, while tansy is effective for aphids, cutworms and cabbage white butterflies.

Recipes

Nettle manure

Macerate 1 kg (2 lb) fresh, chopped nettles in 10 l (qt) rain water for 4–5 days. Filter and dilute to 20% (2 parts manure to 10 parts water) before spraying.

Elder manure

Chop 1 kg (2 lb) elder leaves, flowers, fruit and young stems. Soak in 10 l (qt) water for 3 days. Filter but don't dilute.

Horsetail tea

Cut 200 g (8 oz) fresh horsetail leaves and mix with 10 l (qt) water. Soak for 1 day before boiling for 20 minutes. Let it rest for 24 hours, then filter before spraying.

Establishing insect-repellent plants

The smell of many plants' leaves repels parasites and some diseases. Other plants attract them, pulling them away from neighbouring vegetables or ornamental plants. Below is a table of approximately 20 plant-allies and the parasites and diseases they fight.

Helpful plants	Use for	Plant near
Garlic, chives, shallots, onion	blister beetle	peach tree
	flies	carrot
Lovage	flea beetle	cabbage, turnip, radish
	aphids	beans, lettuce, tomato
Basil	mildew	cucumber, squash
Borage	cabbage white butterfly	cabbage
Nasturtium	whitefly	aubergine (eggplant), cabbage, cucumber, tomato
	mildew	tomato
	aphids	cabbage, cucumber, squash, beans, lettuce, pepper, roses, tomato
Chives	Japanese beetle	potato
	flies	carrot
Coriander (cilantro)	flea beetle	beets, cabbage, turnip, radish
	Japanese beetle	potato
	flies	carrot
Cosmos	cabbage white butterfly	cabbage
Lettuce	flea beetle	cabbage, turnip, radish
Lavender	aphids	roses
Mint	flea beetle	cabbage, turnip radish
	cabbage white butterfly	cabbage
French marigold	whitefly	aubergine (eggplant), cabbage, cucumber, tomato
	flea beetle	cabbage, turnip, radish
	nematodes	tomato
	cabbage white butterfly	cabbage
	aphids	cucumber, squash, spinach, beans, pepper
Parsley	flies	carrot, onion
	aphids	melon, tomato
Horseradish	Japanese beetle	potato
	rust	celery
Rosemary	flea beetle	cabbage, turnip, radish
	flies	carrot, bean
	cabbage white butterfly	cabbage
	aphids	beans, lettuce
Savory	flea beetle	cabbage, turnip, radish
	flies	beans
	cabbage white butterfly	cabbage
	aphids	beans, lettuce
Sage	flea beetle	cabbage, turnip, radish
	flies	carrot
	cabbage white butterfly	cabbage
	aphids	cucumber, squash, lettuce
Common marigold	whitefly	aubergine (eggplant), cabbage, cucumber, tomato
	nematodes	tomato
	aphids	squash, spinach, lettuce, beans, peppers
Tobacco	whitefly	aubergine (eggplant), cabbage, cucumber, tomato
	thrips	gladiolus, pea
Thyme	flea beetle	cabbage, turnip, radish
	slugs	squash, spinach, lettuce, melon
	cabbage white butterfly	cabbage
Tomato	flea beetle	cabbage, turnip, radish

Designing your Garden

You can use the space below to design your garden. If your growing space is small, draw the layout of your March–April crops on the left and your June–July crops on the right, after you have harvested the spring yield.

Indicate where the north lies in relation to your garden. Include unchanging elements such as walls, hedges, paths, cold frames, perennials, fruit trees, herbs, asparagus and artichokes. If these aren't in place yet, indicate where they will be, and pay attention to any tall, overshadowing plants.

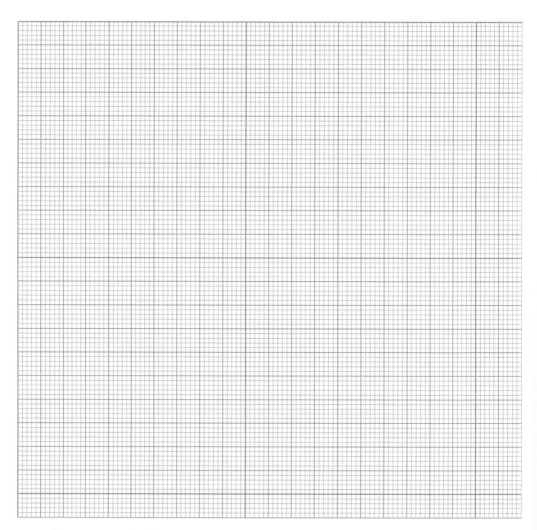

Divide the remaining surface into four equally-sized sections, which will each be occupied by one of the four main categories of vegetable: root, leaf, flower, seed and fruit (see p. 21). Plan the location of your winter crops according to the rules of crop rotation, companion planting and integrating flowers, indicating where the beds will be. When the time is right, just follow your plans and sow or plant your seedlings.

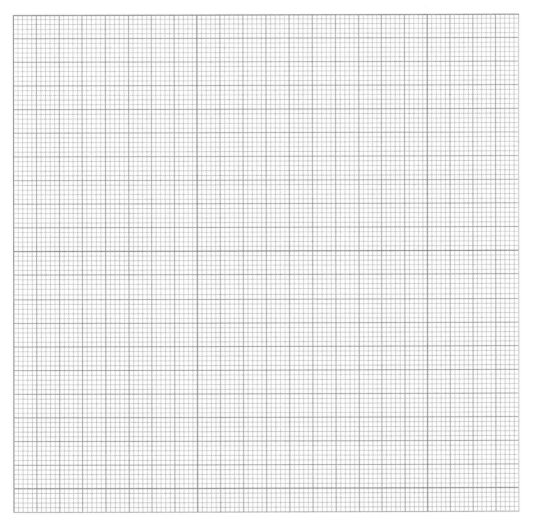

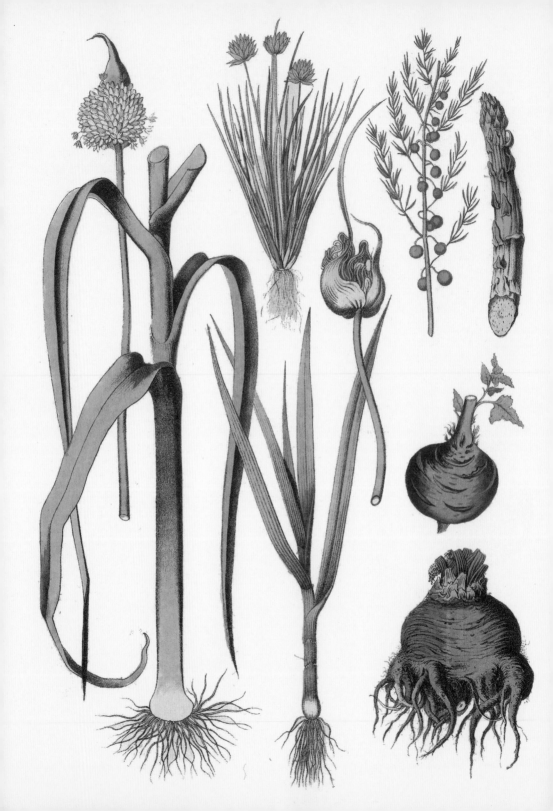

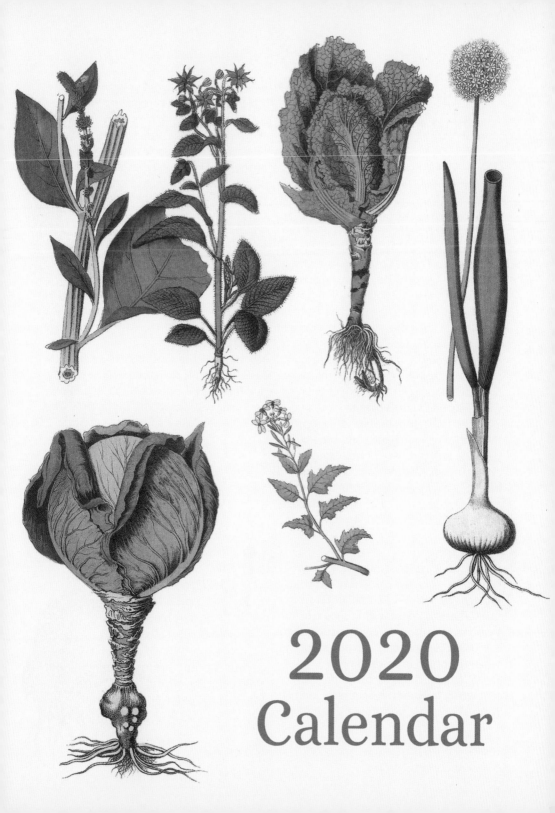

2020
Calendar

How to Use the Calendar

On the following pages, you will find a calendar for the Northern hemisphere and Greenwich Mean Time. It takes into account the main influences from the cosmos, as described in the chapter 'The Moon and the Garden' (pp. 8–33). The vegetables and plants listed are chosen as examples that suit the average growing conditions in France, and can be varied according to your taste, the climate of your garden and its latitude and altitude. Each day we suggest example tasks for tending to leaves, roots, flowers or fruit, according to season, the position of the Sun, and the position of the Moon (ascending or descending in front of particular constellations). You will have to protect your crops from the cold or the heat depending on the climate of your garden and the time of year. The examples given match an *average* climate in France. Take into account your own climate, jumping ahead or postponing tasks as compared to the calendar. If you have frost, delay all planting, pruning and treatments.

Note

It is not always possible – for personal or climatic reasons – to choose the best moment to perform particular gardening tasks. The main consideration should be the motion of the Moon – **always sow when the Moon is ascending, plant and prune when the Moon is descending.**

We have included a blank page every two weeks for you to keep a daily journal. Note everything you do in the garden: which variety of carrots or beans you sow, which day the lettuce came up, when you picked the first tomatoes or beans, when the almond tree blossomed, and when the first cuckoo sang. Don't hesitate to include birthdays. Does someone like a particular plant? Make a note in your calendar to sow or plant this flower at the right time so you can give them a cutting. Your notes will help you to progress your gardening skills and knowledge, and the more notes you take, the more pleasure you will have consulting them.

Remember, all times are given in GMT. If you are not in Britain or Ireland, you need to adjust for your time zone (see p. 37).

Crop tables

You may prefer to plan your tasks differently. Make a list of the plants you want to cultivate and then create a personal calendar of your gardening with the Moon. The crop table on pp. 106–15 offers a range of possibilities.

Calendar key

⊙	the Sun
⊙ ♐	eg. the Sun is in Sagittarius (see p. 18 for constellation symbols)
●	new Moon
◐	first quarter Moon
○	full Moon
◑	last quarter Moon
☊	ascending Moon node
☋	descending Moon node

Note: Do not confuse ascending or descending Moon nodes with the ascending or descending Moon.

Local Times

Times given are *Greenwich Mean Time* (GMT), using 24-hour clock, e.g. 3pm is written 15:00. **No account is taken of daylight saving (summer) time (DST).** Note 00:00 is midnight at the beginning of a date, and 24:00 is midnight at the end of the date. Add (+) or subtract (–) times as below. For countries not listed check local time against GMT.

Europe

Britain, Ireland, Portugal: GMT
    (March 31 to Oct 26, +1^h for DST)
Iceland: GMT (no DST)
Central Europe: +1^h
    (March 31 to Oct 26, +2^h for DST)
Eastern Europe (Finland, etc.): +2^h
    (March 31 to Oct 26, +3^h for DST)
Russia (Moscow) +3^h (no DST)
Georgia: +4^h (no DST)

Africa/Asia

Egypt: add 2^h (no DST)
Israel: add 2^h (March 29 to Oct 26,
    +3^h for DST)
India: add 5½^h (no DST)
Philippines, China: add 8^h (no DST)
Japan, Korea: add 9^h (no DST)

North America

Newfoundland Standard Time: – 3½^h
    (March 10 to Nov 2, – 2½^h for DST)
Atlantic Standard Time: – 4^h
    (March 10 to Nov 2, – 3^h for DST)
Eastern Standard Time: – 5^h
    (March 10 to Nov 2, – 4^h for DST)
Central Standard Time: – 6^h
    (except Saskatchewan March 10 to Nov 2,
    – 5^h for DST)
Mountain Standard Time: – 7^h (except AZ,
    March 10 to Nov 2, – 6^h for DST)
Pacific Standard Time: – 8^h
    (March 10 to Nov 2, – 7^h for DST)
Alaska Standard Time: – 9^h
    (March 10 to Nov 2, – 8^h for DST)
Hawaii Standard Time: – 10^h
    (no DST)
Mexico (CST): –6^h
    (April 7 to Oct 26, –5^h for DST)

January 2020

Ascending moon

Descending moon

☉ ♐ ~~~ 09:40 · · · **Wednesday 1**

Apogee 01:30

◑ 04:45

♓

14:00

♈

12:50

♉

06:40

☊ 23:30

06:02
○ Total eclipse of the Moon 19:22

♊

07:00

♋

18:00

Perigee 20:21

♌

03:50

♍

Thursday 2

Friday 3

Saturday 4

Sunday 5

Monday 6

Tuesday 7

Wednesday 8

Thursday 9

Friday 10

Saturday 11

Sunday 12

Monday 13

Tuesday 14

Wednesday 15

Thursday 16

Happy New Year! Sow cauliflowers (*Serac, Cheddar*) in pots, in a warm place (15–18°C / 60–65°F). When they start to grow thin them, and transplant in a warm place around February 6 or 7.

Do not garden between 08:30 on Jan 1 and 06:30 on Jan 2. Sow head lettuce (*Appia, May Queen*) in a warm place (12–15°C / 55–60°F) in pots, only slightly burying the seeds. Pack down and water lightly. In a cold frame, scatter golden purslane by hand or sow in rows spaced 20 cm (8 in) apart. Keep the soil moist. Harvest in 2 months (March) for delicious salad leaves. Protect lamb's lettuce (mâche), spinach and winter lettuce with a fleece held in place with bricks or planks.

In mild regions, sow broad beans/fava (*Seville Longpods, Aguadulce*) directly into the ground in rows spaced 30–40 cm (just over 1 ft) apart, 5 cm (2 in) deep.

Sow turnips in trays or a cold frame, in rows, every 20 cm (8 in) at 15 °C (60°F) (*Green Globe, Golden Ball, Norfolk Purple*). Aerate frequently and keep the soil moist. Sow white pickling onions (*Paris Silverskin, Barletta Silverskin, de Vaugirard*) directly into the ground in wide rows spaced 20 cm (8 in) apart, dispersing the seeds well. Protect them with a tunnel or cold frame if necessary. Don't thin them, harvest in 2–3 months.

Do not garden between 16:20 on Jan 13 and 01:20 on Jan 14. Plant flowering bare-root shrubs, such as althaea, buddleia, deutzia, forsythia, flowering currant and lilac. Work compost into the roots and spread them out in the hole to encourage them to take well. Place the collar at ground level, fill the hole with soil, pack down and water.

Prepare a plot for planting asparagus crowns in March. Dig trenches 40 cm (1 ½ ft) wide, 25 cm (10 in) deep, spaced 80 cm (2 ½ ft) apart.

On January 13, do not garden after 16:15. Plant bare-root fruit trees and soft-fruit shrubs, adding horn meal and compost to the soil. Support trees with stakes, keep any grafting sites above ground, and bury the base of shrubs. Brush tree trunks to remove moss and lichen, and spray on a winter pest-control treatment.

In mild regions, plant garlic in light soil, in a plot that has not recently been treated with manure or been used for growing beans, peas or a green manure crop from the legume family. Try white garlic (*Messidrome* or *Thermidrome*) or purple garlic (*Germidour*).

▶▶▶

Your notes and observations

January 2020

All times are displayed in GMT using the 24-hour clock

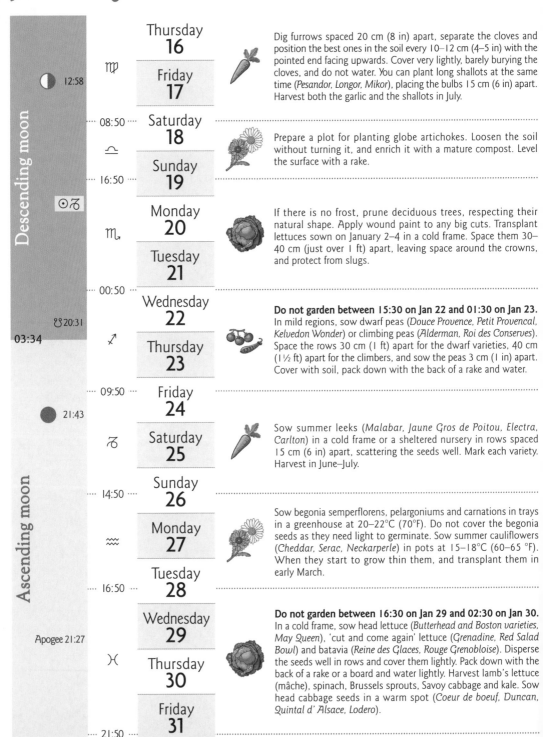

Descending moon

12:58 ◑

♍︎

········ 08:50 ········

♎︎

········ 16:50 ········

☉♑︎

♏︎

········ 00:50 ········

☊ 20:31

03:34

♐︎

········ 09:50 ········

21:43 ●

♑︎

Ascending moon

········ 14:50 ········

♒︎

········ 16:50 ········

Apogee 21:27

♓︎

········ 21:50 ········

Thursday 16

Friday 17

Dig furrows spaced 20 cm (8 in) apart, separate the cloves and position the best ones in the soil every 10–12 cm (4–5 in) with the pointed end facing upwards. Cover very lightly, barely burying the cloves, and do not water. You can plant long shallots at the same time (*Pesandor, Longor, Mikor*), placing the bulbs 15 cm (6 in) apart. Harvest both the garlic and the shallots in July.

Saturday 18

Sunday 19

Prepare a plot for planting globe artichokes. Loosen the soil without turning it, and enrich it with a mature compost. Level the surface with a rake.

Monday 20

Tuesday 21

If there is no frost, prune deciduous trees, respecting their natural shape. Apply wound paint to any big cuts. Transplant lettuces sown on January 2–4 in a cold frame. Space them 30–40 cm (just over 1 ft) apart, leaving space around the crowns, and protect from slugs.

Wednesday 22

Thursday 23

Do not garden between 15:30 on Jan 22 and 01:30 on Jan 23. In mild regions, sow dwarf peas (*Douce Provence, Petit Provençal, Kelvedon Wonder*) or climbing peas (*Alderman, Roi des Conserves*). Space the rows 30 cm (1 ft) apart for the dwarf varieties, 40 cm (1½ ft) apart for the climbers, and sow the peas 3 cm (1 in) apart. Cover with soil, pack down with the back of a rake and water.

Friday 24

Saturday 25

Sow summer leeks (*Malabar, Jaune Gros de Poitou, Electra, Carlton*) in a cold frame or a sheltered nursery in rows spaced 15 cm (6 in) apart, scattering the seeds well. Mark each variety. Harvest in June–July.

Sunday 26

Monday 27

Sow begonia semperflorens, pelargoniums and carnations in trays in a greenhouse at 20–22°C (70°F). Do not cover the begonia seeds as they need light to germinate. Sow summer cauliflowers (*Cheddar, Serac, Neckarperle*) in pots at 15–18°C (60–65 °F). When they start to grow thin them, and transplant them in early March.

Tuesday 28

Wednesday 29

Thursday 30

Do not garden between 16:30 on Jan 29 and 02:30 on Jan 30. In a cold frame, sow head lettuce (*Butterhead and Boston varieties, May Queen*), 'cut and come again' lettuce (*Grenadine, Red Salad Bowl*) and batavia (*Reine des Glaces, Rouge Grenobloise*). Disperse the seeds well in rows and cover them lightly. Pack down with the back of a rake or a board and water lightly. Harvest lamb's lettuce (mâche), spinach, Brussels sprouts, Savoy cabbage and kale. Sow head cabbage seeds in a warm spot (*Coeur de boeuf, Duncan, Quintal d' Alsace, Lodero*).

Friday 31

Your notes and observations

February 2020

Ascending moon

◐ 01:41

♈

Saturday 1

In mild regions, sow broad beans/fava (*Seville Longpods, Aguadulce*) in a plot in rows spaced 30–40 cm (just over 1 ft) apart; in any region, sow peas and mangetout.

Sunday 2

···· 21:50 ····

Monday 3

♉

Tuesday 4

Sow red and yellow onions (*Red Baron, Sturon, Doux de Cévennes, Setton, Hyred*) in a plot in wide rows spaced 30–40 cm (just over 1 ft) apart, and 1–2 cm (½ in) deep. Cover, pack down with the back of a rake and water. When they start to grow, thin them, leaving a plant every 15–20 cm (6–8 in). Harvest from July to September.

Wednesday 5

···· 16:50 ····

☊ 08:59

16:09

♊

Thursday 6

On February 6, do not garden between 04:00 and 14:00. Transplant the cauliflowers sown on January 1 into pots in a warm position. Plant anemone De Caen and ranunculus. Propagate chrysanthemum, fuchsia and pelargonium from cuttings. Plant tuberous begonias and cannas.

Friday 7

···· 16:50 ····

♋

Saturday 8

If there is no frost, plant a hedge of deciduous shrubs, bought either bare-root or in a pot. Work compost into the roots or water the clods. Cut hazel branches to use as stakes.

○ 09:33

···· 03:50 ····

Sunday 9

♌

Monday 10

Do not garden between 15:20 on Feb 10 and 01:20 on Feb 11. When there is no frost, prune framed (espaliered) and free-form fruit trees, preserving the healthiest parts. Spray them with fungicide or a similar alternative. Prune soft-fruit shrubs, actinidias and grapevines. Propagate black and red currants from cuttings.

Perigee 20:27

···· 11:50 ····

Tuesday 11

Descending moon

♍

Wednesday 12

In all regions, plant shallots (*Mikor, Pesandor, Longor*) in loosened soil that has not recently been treated with manure. Space the furrows 25 cm (10 in) apart and position the bulbs 15 cm (6 in) apart, barely covering the tips. Do not water. Plant pink garlic (*Lautrec Wight*), separating the cloves, and covering very lightly. Do not water. Harvest Chinese artichokes, leeks and salsify.

Thursday 13

···· 14:50 ····

Friday 14

♎

Saturday 15

When the hard frosts have ended, take any protection away from globe artichokes, remove sucker shoots, and enrich their plot with compost. Plant bare-root and climbing roses. Transplant the begonias sown January 27–28 into pots. Divide snowdrops.

◐ 22:17

···· 21:50 ····

♏

Sunday 16

Prepare your asparagus plot (see January 11–12). Plant the lettuce sown January 29–31 under shelter. Space the roots 30–40 cm

▶▶▶

Your notes and observations

February 2020

Descending moon

☉≈

♏

05:50

08:53   ☊ 00:11

14:50

♐

Sunday
16

Monday
17

Tuesday
18

Wednesday
19

Thursday
20

(just over 1 ft) apart, leaving space around the crowns, water lightly. Aerate and protect against slugs. In mild weather, use string to mark a straight line for pruning boxwood borders.

Do not garden between 19:10 on Feb 18 and 05:10 on Feb 19. In trays, at 20 °C (70 °F), sow aubergines/eggplants (*Baluroi, Long Purple, Bonica*), sweet peppers (*Gypsy, Gourmet, Doux D'Espagne*) and chilli peppers (*Cayenne, Petit Marseillais, de la Bresse*). Space the seeds 2–3 cm (1 in) apart, lightly cover them, pack down the soil and water. Cover with a cloche and air every day to avoid condensation.

♑

21:50

Friday
21

Saturday
22

In a cold frame, sow carrots (*Touchon, Nandor, Valor*) and radishes (*Gaudry 2, Flamboyant 5, 18 Day*). Mix the two types of seed in the same row: when you harvest the radishes, thin the carrots.

Ascending moon

● 15:31

≈

23:50

Sunday
23

Monday
24

Tuesday
25

In a nursery with plenty of sun or in a cold frame, sow cauliflower (*Serac, Cheddar, Neckarperle, Snow Crown*) and broccoli (*Chevalier, Green Magic, Romanesco*). Space rows 10 cm (4 in) apart and disperse the seeds well. Cover lightly with fine soil, pack down with the back of a rake and water lightly. Plant Busy Lizzie (impatiens) and petunias in pots in a warm spot.

Apogee 11:45

♓

Wednesday
26

Thursday
27

On February 26, do not garden between 06:40 and 16:50. Sow spring spinach (*Palco, America, Viking*) in a plot, 2 cm (1 in) deep, in rows spaced 30 cm (1 ft) apart. Either in a plot or in the nursery, sow head lettuce (*Butterhead varieties, Merveille des Quatre Saisons, May Queen*), batavia (*Reine des Glaces, Rouge Grenobloise*), 'cut and come again' (*Grenadine, Red Salad Bowl*) or Romaine lettuce (*Verte Maraîchère*). You can also sow dandelions, cress and rocket (arugula) in rows spaced 20–30 cm (just under 1 ft) apart. Keep the soil moist until they sprout.

04:50

♈

Friday
28

Saturday
29

In a warm greenhouse at 18–20 °C (65–70 °F), sow tomatoes (*Lemon Boy, Fandango, Super Marmande, Saint Pierre, Pyros*).

Your notes and observations

March 2020

Ascending moon

◐ 19:57

♉

♍ 14:58

01:34

♊

☽ 17:47

Perigee 06:36

⊙ ♓

Descending moon

♎

♏

◐ 09:34

♐

04:50

Sunday
1

Monday
2

Tuesday
3

01:50

Wednesday
4

Thursday
5

03:50

Friday
6

Saturday
7

14:50

Sunday
8

Monday
9

21:50

Tuesday
10

Wednesday
11

Thursday
12

22:50

Friday
13

04:50

Saturday
14

Sunday
15

11:50

Monday
16

In a warm spot, in trays filled with a light compost, sow Monarch celeriac. Cover the seeds lightly, pack down with a board and keep the soil damp until the seedlings sprout. In the nursery, sow leeks for autumn harvest (*Jaune Gros du Poitou, Malabar, Pancho, Hannibal*). Thin the seedlings after germination, keeping them 5 cm (2 in) apart. In a plot, sow stratified root chervil (seeds that have been layered with damp sand and stored in a cold spot for 2 months to encourage germination).

On March 4, do not garden between 10:00 and 20:00.
Prune climbing roses, cutting back bushes close to the ground, and trimming tall varieties. Remove sucker shoots from globe artichokes. In the nursery transplant the cauliflowers, and in pots the pelargoniums, sown on January 27–28.

Plant asparagus by spreading the crowns over mounds. Fill the trench with soil, burying the roots 5 cm (2 in) deep, and water. Plant container-grown evergreen shrubs.

Prune pip-fruit trees and vines. Prune peach trees as they start to flower, and olive trees. Remove excess growth from the canopy and from the shady base, to let in light and air. Hoe the peas and broad beans (fava) sown on February 2, supporting climbing varieties with canes.

On March 10, do not garden between 01:40 and 11:40.
In rows spaced 80 cm (2 ½ ft) apart, plant early germinating potatoes (*Belle de Fontenay, Abbot, Maris Bard*). Place them every 35 cm (14 in) and 10 cm (4 in) deep with shoots facing upwards, and cover. When the leaves are 25 cm (10 in) tall, earth them up. Plant Chinese and Jerusalem artichokes and horseradish. Thin the carrots sown on February 21–22.

Under cover, plant the cauliflowers sown on January 1. Transplant the cauliflowers, and broccoli sown on February 23–24, and thin the Busy Lizzie (impatiens) sown on the same day, to one plant every 5 cm (2 in). Prune summer-flowering shrubs, clematis and climbing roses.

Blanch dandelions. Plant or divide chives, tarragon, sorrel and rhubarb, adding compost. Plant asparagus. Transplant the head cabbage sown on February 1 in a cold frame. Thin the spinach and dandelions, and plant the lettuce, sown on February 26–28.

Graft split or scaled fruit trees.

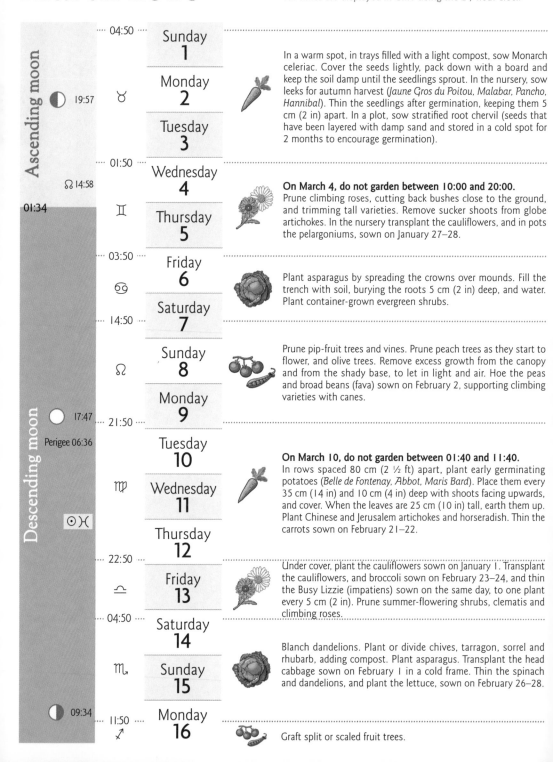

Your notes and observations

March 2020

Descending moon ☊ 01:59

◐ 09:34 ♏ 11:50

15:00

Ascending moon

● 09:28
Apogee 15:39

Spring Equinox 03:49

☊ 16:51

Monday 16

♏ 11:50

Tuesday 17

♐

Wednesday 18

20:50

Do not garden between 20:00 on Mar 16 and 06:00 on Mar 17. In trays, at 20 °C (70 °F), sow aubergines/eggplants (*Baluroi, Long Purple, Bonica*), sweet peppers (*Gypsy, Gourmet, Doux D'Espagne*) and chilli peppers (*Cayenne, Petit Marseillais, de la Bresse*), covering the seeds lightly. Pack down, water and cover with a cloche. Air every day to avoid condensation. Sow tomatoes in a greenhouse at 18–20 °C (65–70 °F).

Thursday 19

♑

Friday 20

03:50

In a plot, sow carrots (*Early Nantes, Adelaide, Flyaway*) in rows spaced 30 cm (1 ft) apart, 2 cm (1 in) deep. Pack down and water. Sow radishes and in wide furrows sow beets (*Detroit, Egyptian*).

Saturday 21

♒

Sunday 22

05:50

Sow hardy annuals, such as fragrant alyssa, cornflower, clarkia, godetia, larkspur, Damascus nigellas, Californian poppy and strawflower in beds. Scatter the seeds well, cover lightly, pack down and water lightly. Sow sweet peas seeds in holes, with a cane support.

Monday 23

Tuesday 24

♓

Wednesday 25

10:50

On March 24, do not garden between 04:30 and 14:30. In a nursery with good sun exposure sow head cabbages (*Quintal d'Alsace, Red Express, Lodero*) and Brussels sprouts for harvesting in autumn (*Rubine, Jadeh Cross*). Sow frisée chicory or curly endive (*Très Fine Maraîchère, Natacha*) in pots at 25 °C (77 °F) for rapid growth. Also sow rocket (arugula), parsley and chervil.

Thursday 26

♈

Friday 27

10:50

Sow peas, mangetout and broad beans (fava) in rows spaced 30–40 cm (just over 1 ft) apart. Hoe when they sprout. At 20–25 °C (70–77 °F) sow melon seeds and physalis in pots.

Saturday 28

♉

Sunday 29

Monday 30

08:50

In a plot, sow round or long radishes in rows, space the seeds well apart. Sow parsnips (*Half-long Guernsey*) in rows spaced 30–40 cm (just over 1 ft) apart. In the nursery, sow leeks (*Malabar, Carantan, Electra*). When they sprout, thin them to one plant every 5 cm (2 in). Harvest both parsnips and leeks in the autumn.

Tuesday 31

♊

On March 31, do not garden between 11:50 and 21:50.

Your notes and observations

April 2020

Ascending moon
09:13   ◐ 10:21

♊

Wednesday
1

Transplant the seedlings sown on January 27–28: carnations in the nursery, begonias in pots and cauliflowers in a plot. Transplant the petunias sown on February 23–24 in pots.

···· 12:50 ····

Thursday
2

♋

Friday
3

Mow and scarify the lawn. Apply a nitrogen-rich fertiliser. Replant the borders. Plant parsley, rosemary, sage, chervil and thyme in beds or pots. Plant the head cabbages sown on February 1 in a plot.

···· 00:50 ····

Saturday
4

♌

Sunday
5

Plant climbing strawberries, and soft-fruit shrubs (gooseberries, blackcurrants and raspberries), adding compost. Bury the base of the shrub stems and water. Transplant the aubergines (eggplants), chillies and peppers sown on February 18–20 and the tomatoes sown on February 29.

Descending moon

···· 09:50 ····

Monday
6

On April 7, do not garden between 13:10 and 23:20.
Plant ocas (New Zealand yam) in pots in a warm spot. Plant main-crop potatoes (*Charlotte, Roseval, Ratte*). Earth them up when the foliage is around 25 cm (10 in) high. Plant the leeks sown on January 25–26 in rows spaced 30 cm (1 ft) apart, every 10 cm (4 in). Transplant the celeriac sown on March 1–3 for the first time. Thin the beets and carrots sown on March 19–20.

Perigee 18:15
○ 02:35

♍

Tuesday
7

Wednesday
8

···· 09:50 ····

Thursday
9

♎

Plant perennials and flowering shrubs. Prune any spring-flowering shrubs that have finished. Remove old, weak and dead wood at the base of branches to aerate the canopy. Transplant the pelargoniums sown on January 27–28 again.

Friday
10

···· 14:50 ····

Saturday
11

♏

When the chicory and endive sown on March 24–26 has 5 strong leaves, transplant it under cover. Space each plant 10 cm (4 in) apart in every direction, aerate often and protect from slugs. In the nursery, transplant the head cabbage and Brussels sprouts sown on the same date.

Sunday
12

···· 19:50 ····

☊ 02:59

Do not garden between 22:00 on April 12 and 08:00 on April 13.
Sow courgette (zucchini), marrow or squash in pots of acid-rich compost: 3 seeds per pot at 18–20 °C (65–70 °F), and cucumbers at 20–25 °C (70–75 °F). Pack down and water. When they sprout, keep the best plant of each batch. Graft fruit-tree crowns using cuttings taken last winter. Sow pea seeds (*Kelvedon Wonder*).

Monday
13

20:18

Ascending moon

♐

Tuesday
14

◐ 22:56

···· 02:50 ····

Wednesday
15

♑

Next to the leeks, sow carrots (*Lisse de Meaux, Jaune du Doubs, Touchon*) to fight flies and ringworm. Dig two wide furrows, spacing the seeds well apart to reduce thinning. Harvest August to September.

Thursday
16

Your notes and observations

April 2020

Ascending moon

♅

Thursday 16

Sow turnips (*de Nancy, Atlantic, Milan Purple Top, Norfolk Purple*) in rows spaced 20 cm (8 in) apart. Cover lightly, pack down and water. Sow onions (*Red Baron, Red Brunswick, Sturon, Setton*) in rows spaced 30 cm (1 ft) apart.

···· 09:50 ····

Friday 17

☉♈ ♒

Saturday 18

Sow hardy annuals, such as fragrant alyssa, cornflower, clarkia, larkspur, Damascus nigellas, Californian poppy and morning glory along the borders of vegetable plots and in gaps in flowerbeds. Cover seeds lightly, pack down with the back of a rake and water lightly to avoid disturbing the seeds.

···· 11:50 ····

Sunday 19

Apogee 19:12

Monday 20

On April 20, do not garden between 14:10 and 24:00.
In a cold frame or nursery with good sun exposure (soil temperature above 11 °C/50 °F) sow celery (*Tall Utah, Giant Red*). Sow Swiss chard (*Bright Yellow, Lucullus*) in beds, in rows spaced 40 cm (1 ½ ft) apart, watering the soil before seeding if dry. Sow heat-hardy varieties of batavia, 'cut and come again' and head lettuce. Sow bulb fennel (*Florence, Orion*) under a tunnel or in a well-exposed, sunny nursery. Keep the soil moist and thin the seedlings.

♓

Tuesday 21

···· 16:50 ····

Wednesday 22

● 02:25

♈

Thursday 23

In mild regions, sow melon and cucumber seeds in a plot, in holes; everywhere else, sow them in pots at 20–22 °C (70–75 °F).

···· 16:50 ····

Friday 24

Saturday 25

On April 27, do not garden between 12:50 and 22:50.
Sow more turnips (*Golden Ball, Green Globe*). Sow salsify in a plot, spacing the seeds 20 cm (8 in) apart. Cover the seeds lightly, pack down and water. Thin when the plants have 2–3 leaves. Sow parsnips (*Half-long Guernsey*) in rows spaced 30–40 cm (just over 1 ft) apart. Bury the seeds 1 cm (½ in) deep, pack down and water.

♉

Sunday 26

☊17:54 ···· 14:50 ····

Monday 27

15:21

Tuesday 28

♊

Plant begonias, cannas, dahlias, gladiolas and perennials in flowerbeds; in pots and window boxes, plant annuals in mild regions, and elsewhere protect them on cool nights. Plant the cauliflowers and broccoli sown on February 23–24 in a plot, and transplant the petunias and Busy Lizzy (impatiens) sown at the same time into pots.

Wednesday 29

Descending moon

···· 18:50 ····

♋

Thursday 30

Plant the chicory sown March 24–26 in a plot, leaving 30–40 cm (just over 1 ft) space around each plant. Harvest them in June/July, after blanching. Prune evergreen hedges, topiary and boxwood borders.

◑ 20:38

Your notes and observations

May 2020

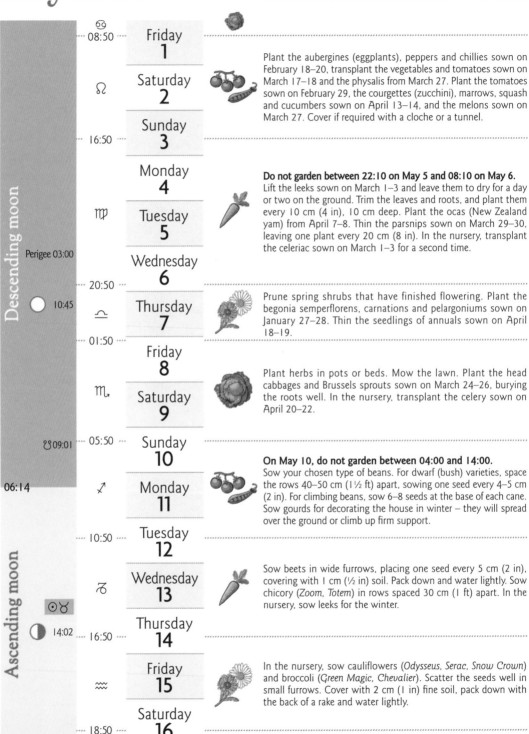

Descending moon

♋ 08:50

Friday 1

Plant the aubergines (eggplants), peppers and chillies sown on February 18–20, transplant the vegetables and tomatoes sown on March 17–18 and the physalis from March 27. Plant the tomatoes sown on February 29, the courgettes (zucchini), marrows, squash and cucumbers sown on April 13–14, and the melons sown on March 27. Cover if required with a cloche or a tunnel.

♌

Saturday 2

16:50

Sunday 3

Monday 4

Do not garden between 22:10 on May 5 and 08:10 on May 6.
Lift the leeks sown on March 1–3 and leave them to dry for a day or two on the ground. Trim the leaves and roots, and plant them every 10 cm (4 in), 10 cm deep. Plant the ocas (New Zealand yam) from April 7–8. Thin the parsnips sown on March 29–30, leaving one plant every 20 cm (8 in). In the nursery, transplant the celeriac sown on March 1–3 for a second time.

♍

Tuesday 5

Perigee 03:00

Wednesday 6

○ 10:45

20:50

♎

Thursday 7

Prune spring shrubs that have finished flowering. Plant the begonia semperflorens, carnations and pelargoniums sown on January 27–28. Thin the seedlings of annuals sown on April 18–19.

01:50

Friday 8

Plant herbs in pots or beds. Mow the lawn. Plant the head cabbages and Brussels sprouts sown on March 24–26, burying the roots well. In the nursery, transplant the celery sown on April 20–22.

♏

Saturday 9

☊ 09:01

05:50

Sunday 10

On May 10, do not garden between 04:00 and 14:00.
Sow your chosen type of beans. For dwarf (bush) varieties, space the rows 40–50 cm (1½ ft) apart, sowing one seed every 4–5 cm (2 in). For climbing beans, sow 6–8 seeds at the base of each cane. Sow gourds for decorating the house in winter – they will spread over the ground or climb up firm support.

06:14

♐

Monday 11

10:50

Tuesday 12

Ascending moon

♑

Wednesday 13

Sow beets in wide furrows, placing one seed every 5 cm (2 in), covering with 1 cm (½ in) soil. Pack down and water lightly. Sow chicory (*Zoom, Totem*) in rows spaced 30 cm (1 ft) apart. In the nursery, sow leeks for the winter.

☉♉

◑ 14:02

16:50

Thursday 14

♒

Friday 15

In the nursery, sow cauliflowers (*Odysseus, Serac, Snow Crown*) and broccoli (*Green Magic, Chevalier*). Scatter the seeds well in small furrows. Cover with 2 cm (1 in) fine soil, pack down with the back of a rake and water lightly.

18:50

Saturday 16

Your notes and observations

May 2020

Ascending moon

♒︎

18:50

Saturday 16

Sow fast-growing annuals to fill gaps in flowerbeds and borders. Cover the seeds lightly and water gently to avoid disturbing them.

Sunday 17

Apogee 07:51

♓︎

Monday 18

On May 18, do not garden between 02:50 and 12:50.
Like every month when the moon is in Pisces, sow salad leaves: curly endive, head lettuce, batavia, 'cut and come again', Swiss chard, rocket (arugula), purslane or mesclun. You can also sow cardoon in a plot, in holes spaced 1 m (3 ft) all around, enriching the soil with ripe compost. In the nursery, sow Brussels sprouts (*Rubine, Jade Cross*) and Savoy cabbage (*January King, Vertus, Pontoise*) for the winter.

Tuesday 19

23:50

Wednesday 20

♈︎

In holes enriched with compost, reseed courgettes (zucchini), marrows, squash, cucumber and melons.

Thursday 21

22:50

Friday 22

17:38

♉︎

On May 24, do not garden between 12:40 and 22:40.
Sow carrots for the winter (*Chantenay, Flyaway, Maestro, Purple Haze*) and radishes for the summer and autumn (*China Rose, April Cross*). Thin the seedlings to one every 5 cm (2 in).

Saturday 23

Sunday 24

☊21:34

20:50

Monday 25

21:13

♊︎

Divide spring bulbs, including daffodils (narcissus), tulips and hyacinths, when their leaves are yellow. Keep the best plants, storing them in a dry place or planting them somewhere different. Plant arum lilies. Propagate flowering shrubs (lavander, lilac). In pots or flowerbeds, plants the petunias and Busy Lizzies (impatiens) sown on February 23–24.

Tuesday 26

00:50

Wednesday 27

♋︎

Thin the leeks, keeping a strong plant every 40 cm (1½ ft). In rows spaced 50 cm (2 ft) apart, plant the celery and fennel sown on April 20–22. Space the celery 30–40 cm (just over 1 ft) apart, and the fennel 20 cm (8 in) apart.

Thursday 28

13:50

Descending moon

Friday 29

♌︎

Prune the tomatoes, marrows, squash, courgettes (zucchini), cucumbers and melons that are already in plots. Plant the aubergines (eggplants), peppers, chillies and tomatoes sown on March 17–18, the physalis sown on March 27, and the cucumbers and melons sown in pots on April 23–24. Thin apples and pears, keeping the most attractive cuttings for a bouquet.

03:29

Saturday 30

01:50

♍︎

Sunday 31

Plant the celeriac sown on March 1–3, leaving 40 cm (1½ ft) all around. Dig up early potatoes as required.

Your notes and observations

June 2020

All times are displayed in GMT. In UK/Ireland add 1 hour for BST

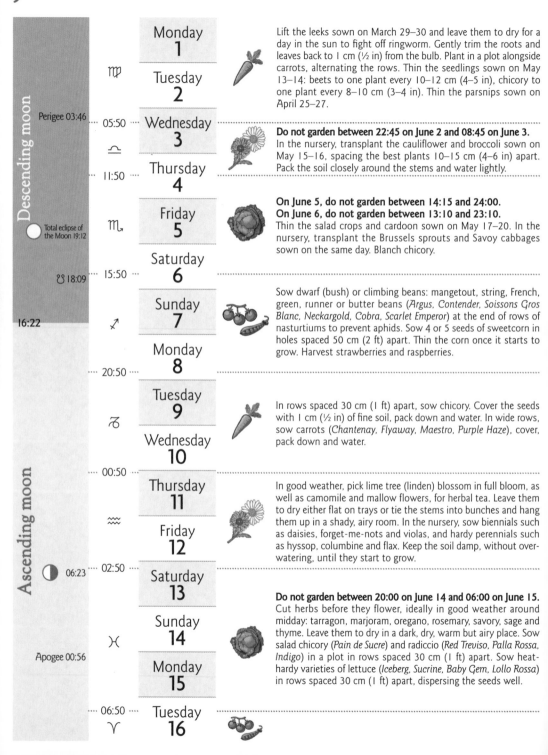

Descending moon

Perigee 03:46

℞ 18:09

16:22

Ascending moon

Apogee 00:56

♍	
05:50	
♎	
11:50	
♏	
15:50	
♐	
20:50	
♑	
00:50	
♒	
02:50	
♓	
06:50	
♈	

Total eclipse of the Moon 19:12

◐ 06:23

Monday 1

Tuesday 2

Lift the leeks sown on March 29–30 and leave them to dry for a day in the sun to fight off ringworm. Gently trim the roots and leaves back to 1 cm (½ in) from the bulb. Plant in a plot alongside carrots, alternating the rows. Thin the seedlings sown on May 13–14: beets to one plant every 10–12 cm (4–5 in), chicory to one plant every 8–10 cm (3–4 in). Thin the parsnips sown on April 25–27.

Wednesday 3

Thursday 4

Do not garden between 22:45 on June 2 and 08:45 on June 3.
In the nursery, transplant the cauliflower and broccoli sown on May 15–16, spacing the best plants 10–15 cm (4–6 in) apart. Pack the soil closely around the stems and water lightly.

Friday 5

Saturday 6

On June 5, do not garden between 14:15 and 24:00.
On June 6, do not garden between 13:10 and 23:10.
Thin the salad crops and cardoon sown on May 17–20. In the nursery, transplant the Brussels sprouts and Savoy cabbages sown on the same day. Blanch chicory.

Sunday 7

Monday 8

Sow dwarf (bush) or climbing beans: mangetout, string, French, green, runner or butter beans (*Argus, Contender, Soissons Gros Blanc, Neckargold, Cobra, Scarlet Emperor*) at the end of rows of nasturtiums to prevent aphids. Sow 4 or 5 seeds of sweetcorn in holes spaced 50 cm (2 ft) apart. Thin the corn once it starts to grow. Harvest strawberries and raspberries.

Tuesday 9

Wednesday 10

In rows spaced 30 cm (1 ft) apart, sow chicory. Cover the seeds with 1 cm (½ in) of fine soil, pack down and water. In wide rows, sow carrots (*Chantenay, Flyaway, Maestro, Purple Haze*), cover, pack down and water.

Thursday 11

Friday 12

In good weather, pick lime tree (linden) blossom in full bloom, as well as camomile and mallow flowers, for herbal tea. Leave them to dry either flat on trays or tie the stems into bunches and hang them up in a shady, airy room. In the nursery, sow biennials such as daisies, forget-me-nots and violas, and hardy perennials such as hyssop, columbine and flax. Keep the soil damp, without over-watering, until they start to grow.

Saturday 13

Sunday 14

Monday 15

Do not garden between 20:00 on June 14 and 06:00 on June 15.
Cut herbs before they flower, ideally in good weather around midday: tarragon, marjoram, oregano, rosemary, savory, sage and thyme. Leave them to dry in a dark, dry, warm but airy place. Sow salad chicory (*Pain de Sucre*) and radiccio (*Red Treviso, Palla Rossa, Indigo*) in a plot in rows spaced 30 cm (1 ft) apart. Sow heat-hardy varieties of lettuce (*Iceberg, Sucrine, Baby Gem, Lollo Rossa*) in rows spaced 30 cm (1 ft) apart, dispersing the seeds well.

Tuesday 16

Your notes and observations

June

June 2020

Ascending moon

06:50 · · · · Tuesday **16**

Y Wednesday **17**

Sow 3 grains of cucumber or courgette (zucchini) in holes enriched with compost.

06:50 · · · · Thursday **18**

X Friday **19**

Saturday **20**

Summer Solstice 21:43

Dig a wide, shallow furrow and scatter beet seeds (*Detroit, Egyptian, Chioggia*). Cover them, pack down and water lightly. Sow radishes for the winter (*China Rose, Violet de Gournay*) and swedes (rutabaga) in rows spaced 30–40 cm (just over 1 ft) apart. When they start to grow, thin the radishes to one plant every 10–15 cm (4–6 in) and the swedes to one every 30 cm (1ft).

☋04:23
Total eclipse of the Sun 06:41
☉Ⅱ

03:50 · · · · Sunday **21**

03:54

Ⅱ Monday **22**

On June 21, do not garden between 00:00 and 11:40.
Prune shrubs that have finished flowering. Propagate linneas (beauty bush) and Russian sage. Divide wisteria, campsis and rhododendrons. Plant the broccoli sown on May 15–16, leaving 60 cm (2 ft) all around. Bury the base of the stems, pack down and water copiously.

06:50 · · · · Tuesday **23**

♋ Wednesday **24**

Thin the Swiss chard sown on May 17–20. Tidy up any places invaded by unwanted thistles, brambles or sloes. Pull them up or cut them back as low as possible so the summer heat weakens their roots.

19:50 · · · ·

Descending moon

Thursday **25**

♌ Friday **26**

Prune any vigorously growing apples and pear trees, or vine crops, including frame (espaliered) trees, removing any unproductive or overly long branches. Prune tomato suckers, excessive or fruitless growth on marrow and pumpkin vines, and cucumber, aubergine (eggplant) and pepper shoots to encourage fruit growth.

07:50 · · · · Saturday **27**

◑ 08:15 Sunday **28**

♍ Monday **29**

Do not garden between 21:20 on June 29 and 07:20 on June 30.
Plant the leeks sown on May 13–14. Thin the carrots and chicory sown on June 9–10. Harvest early potatoes. When their leaves are yellow, pull up garlic, onions and shallots. Let them dry in the sun for one day. To keep your garlic white, cover the bulbs of one row with the tops of another. Store them in an airy room.

Perigee 02:20

12:50 · · · · Tuesday **30**

♎

Plant the cauliflowers sown on May 15–16, spacing them 60–70 cm (2 ft) all around. Pack the soil closely around the roots and

▶▶▶

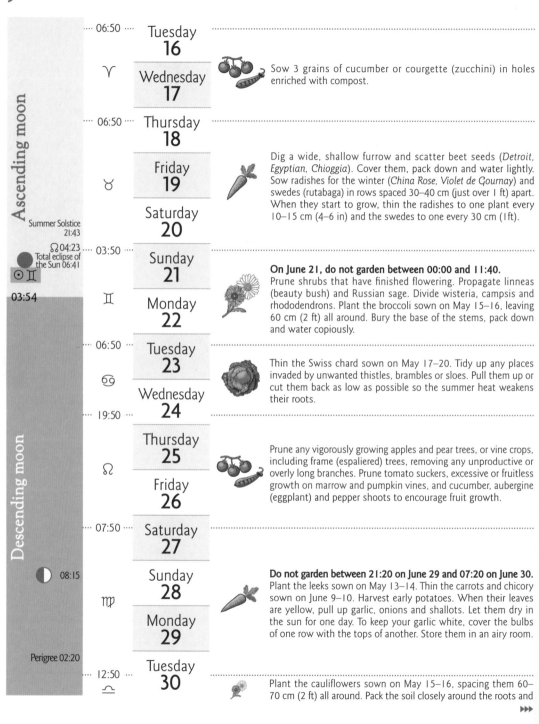

Your notes and observations

July 2020

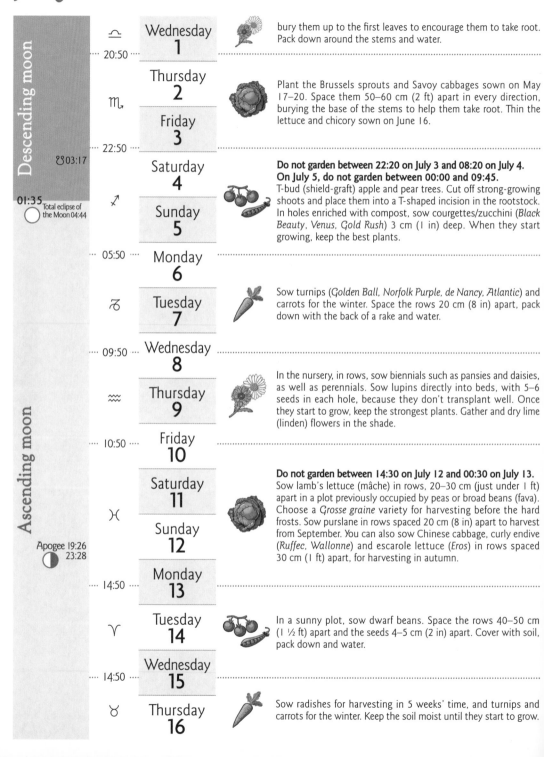

Descending moon

☊ 03:17

01:35
◯ Total eclipse of the Moon 04:44

Ascending moon

Apogee 19:26
◐ 23:28

♎︎
20:50

Wednesday 1

bury them up to the first leaves to encourage them to take root. Pack down around the stems and water.

Thursday 2

♏︎

Friday 3

22:50

Plant the Brussels sprouts and Savoy cabbages sown on May 17–20. Space them 50–60 cm (2 ft) apart in every direction, burying the base of the stems to help them take root. Thin the lettuce and chicory sown on June 16.

Saturday 4

♐︎

Sunday 5

05:50

Do not garden between 22:20 on July 3 and 08:20 on July 4. On July 5, do not garden between 00:00 and 09:45.
T-bud (shield-graft) apple and pear trees. Cut off strong-growing shoots and place them into a T-shaped incision in the rootstock. In holes enriched with compost, sow courgettes/zucchini (*Black Beauty, Venus, Gold Rush*) 3 cm (1 in) deep. When they start growing, keep the best plants.

Monday 6

♑︎

Tuesday 7

09:50

Sow turnips (*Golden Ball, Norfolk Purple, de Nancy, Atlantic*) and carrots for the winter. Space the rows 20 cm (8 in) apart, pack down with the back of a rake and water.

Wednesday 8

♒︎

Thursday 9

10:50

In the nursery, in rows, sow biennials such as pansies and daisies, as well as perennials. Sow lupins directly into beds, with 5–6 seeds in each hole, because they don't transplant well. Once they start to grow, keep the strongest plants. Gather and dry lime (linden) flowers in the shade.

Friday 10

Saturday 11

♓︎

Sunday 12

14:50

Do not garden between 14:30 on July 12 and 00:30 on July 13.
Sow lamb's lettuce (mâche) in rows, 20–30 cm (just under 1 ft) apart in a plot previously occupied by peas or broad beans (fava). Choose a *Grosse graine* variety for harvesting before the hard frosts. Sow purslane in rows spaced 20 cm (8 in) apart to harvest from September. You can also sow Chinese cabbage, curly endive (*Ruffec, Wallonne*) and escarole lettuce (*Eros*) in rows spaced 30 cm (1 ft) apart, for harvesting in autumn.

Monday 13

♈︎

Tuesday 14

In a sunny plot, sow dwarf beans. Space the rows 40–50 cm (1 ½ ft) apart and the seeds 4–5 cm (2 in) apart. Cover with soil, pack down and water.

Wednesday 15

14:50

♉︎

Thursday 16

Sow radishes for harvesting in 5 weeks' time, and turnips and carrots for the winter. Keep the soil moist until they start to grow.

Your notes and observations

July 2020

Ascending moon

♉	Thursday **16**
	Friday **17**
☊ 12:32 · · · 11:50 · · · ·	Saturday **18**

11:51

Descending moon

♊	Sunday **19**
⊙♋ 17:32 · · · 13:50 · · · ·	Monday **20**
♋	Tuesday **21**
· · · 02:50 · · · ·	Wednesday **22**
♌	Thursday **23**
· · · 12:50 · · · ·	Friday **24**
Perigree 04:53 ♍	Saturday **25**
	Sunday **26**
◑ 12:32 · · · 18:50 · · · ·	Monday **27**
♎	Tuesday **28**
· · · 01:50 · · · ·	Wednesday **29**
♏	Thursday **30**
☋ 09:32 · · · 07:50 · · · · ♐	Friday **31**

On July 18, do not garden between 07:30 and 17:30.
Sow radishes for the winter (*China Rose, Black Radish and Violet de Gournay*) in furrows spaced 20–30 cm (just under 1 ft) apart, scattering the seeds well. Cover with soil, pack down and water. When they start to grow keep one plant every 10–15 cm (4–6 in). You can also sow swedes/rutabagas (*Wilhelmsburger, Brora*).

Propagate bay (laurel) cuttings in water, then plant in a pot when the roots appear. Propagate Indian lilac (neem) cuttings directly into a pot or a cold frame. In the nursery, transplant the biennials and perennials sown on June 11–13.

Blanch curly endive and escarole lettuce as required by placing them under an opaque cloche and harvesting them in 10–12 days when they will be sweeter and more tender.

Prune any vigorously growing apple and pear trees, including frame (espaliered) trees. Prune tomato suckers and any excess leaf growth of marrows and pumpkins. Prepare and enrich planting compost for strawberries, ready for planting on August 19–20.

On July 25, do not garden between 00:00 and 10:00.
Prepare a plot for sowing onions on August 12–14 that has not been recently manured and has not been used for growing beans or peas this year. Pull up garlic, shallots and onions and let them dry in the sun for one day before storing in a dry, well-ventilated room. Dig up potatoes for storage. Thin the turnips and carrots sown on July 7 and the beets sown on June 18–20.

Plant or divide irises and daylilies (*Hemerocallis*) to a sunny new bed, keeping only the most beautiful foliage. Plant autumn-flowering bulbs, such as colchicum, crocus, cyclamen, saffron and sternbergia.

If you need to sow a new lawn, prepare the soil now for sowing in September. Dig and refine the soil and even out the surface. Thin the curly endive, lamb's lettuce (mâche), escarole and Chinese cabbage sown July 11–13.

On July 31, do not garden between 04:30 and 14:30.

▶▶▶

Your notes and observations

- first Big leaf Wed. 22
- Identify 1 male
- pruned tomatoes
-

August 2020

Descending moon
08:44

♐

Saturday
1

T-bud (shield-graft) apple, pear and peach trees. Cut off a strong-growing shoot with several buds, select a healthy bud and trim back. Slip the bud into a T-cut made in the rootstock, then bind with raffia. If the petiole falls off two weeks later, the graft has been successful. Sow dwarf green beans in warm growing regions.

···· 13:50 ····

Sunday
2

○ 15:58

♑

Monday
3

Sow radishes for winter (*China Rose, April Cross, Violet de Gournay*) directly into plots in rows spaced 20–30 cm (just under 1 ft) apart. Disperse the seeds well, cover, pack down and water.

Tuesday
4

···· 17:50 ····

♒

Wednesday
5

T-bud (shield-graft) wild (dog) roses. Make a T-shaped incision in the rootstock. Carefully cut off strong-growing shoots for grafting, trimming them back to 2 cm (1 in) above and below a good bud. Carefully remove excess woody material from around the bud, and insert it into the T-shaped slot. Bind with raffia. In the nursery, sow pansies, violas and daisies in rows spaced 10 cm (4 in) apart, labelling each variety.

Thursday
6

···· 18:50 ····

Ascending moon

♓

Friday
7

On August 9, do not garden between 08:45 and 10:45.
Sow frost-hardy lamb's lettuce (mâche) varieties (*Coquille de Louvier, Verte de Cambrai*), as well as Chinese cabbage (*Granaat, Yuki, bok-choy*). Sow spinach (*Viroflay, Amazon, Palco*) in rows spaced 20–30 cm (just under 1 ft) apart. Sow 'cut and come again' lettuce to harvest before the hard frosts or winter varieties (*Verpia, Marvel of Four Seasons, Valdor, Rouge Di'Hiver*) to harvest in spring. In the nursery, sow head cabbage (*Cœur de bœuf, Protovoy*). You will thin all of these on August 26.

Saturday
8

Apogee 13:46

Sunday
9

···· 22:50 ····

☉♌

♈

Monday
10

Pick beans for shelling to eat fresh or to dry. Harvest tomato seeds, put them in a glass and let them grow mouldy. Wash them, dry them and store them in a dry place.

◑ 16:44

Tuesday
11

···· 22:50 ····

♉

Wednesday
12

On August 14, do not garden between 14:20 and 24:00.
Sow turnips (*De Nancy, Atlantic, Norfolk Purple, Green Globe, Golden Ball*) in rows spaced 20 cm (8 in) apart. Cover, pack down and water. Keep the soil moist until they start to grow. In mild growing regions, in the nursery, sow onions (*Long Red Florence, Spanish*) and white pickling onions (*Paris Silverskin, Barletta Silverskin, de Vaugirard*). A few days after they start to sprout, thin them to one plant every 5 cm (2 in).

Thursday
13

☊ 19:23 ···· 20:50 ····

Friday
14

20:39
Descending moon

♊

Saturday
15

Propagate roses. Take 15 cm (6 in) long cuttings from this year's growth. Remove leaves and thorns from the base of the stems and bury them 10 cm (4 in) deep in a light mix of sand and compost in a shaded cold frame to protect them over the winter.

Sunday
16

···· 23:50 ····

Your notes and observations

August 2020

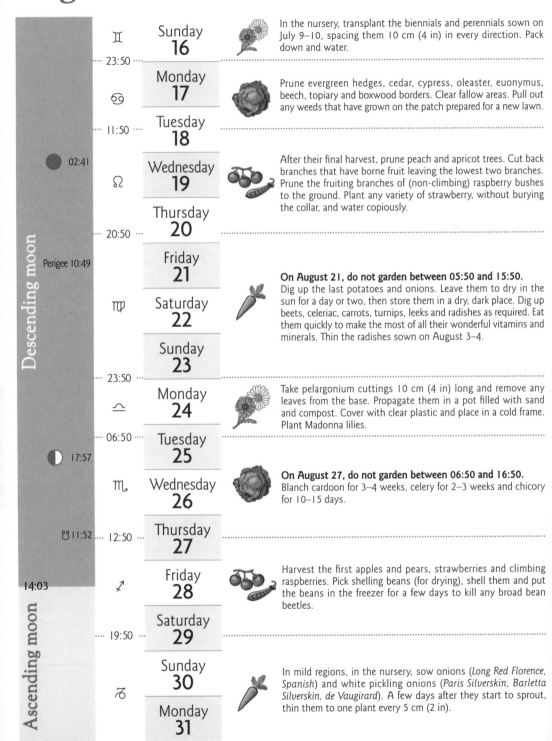

Descending moon

♊ — Sunday **16** — 23:50

In the nursery, transplant the biennials and perennials sown on July 9–10, spacing them 10 cm (4 in) in every direction. Pack down and water.

♋ — Monday **17**

Prune evergreen hedges, cedar, cypress, oleaster, euonymus, beech, topiary and boxwood borders. Clear fallow areas. Pull out any weeds that have grown on the patch prepared for a new lawn.

11:50 — Tuesday **18**

● 02:41 — ♌ — Wednesday **19**

After their final harvest, prune peach and apricot trees. Cut back branches that have borne fruit leaving the lowest two branches. Prune the fruiting branches of (non-climbing) raspberry bushes to the ground. Plant any variety of strawberry, without burying the collar, and water copiously.

Thursday **20** — 20:50

Perigee 10:49 — Friday **21**

On August 21, do not garden between 05:50 and 15:50.
Dig up the last potatoes and onions. Leave them to dry in the sun for a day or two, then store them in a dry, dark place. Dig up beets, celeriac, carrots, turnips, leeks and radishes as required. Eat them quickly to make the most of all their wonderful vitamins and minerals. Thin the radishes sown on August 3–4.

♍ — Saturday **22**

Sunday **23** — 23:50

♎ — Monday **24**

Take pelargonium cuttings 10 cm (4 in) long and remove any leaves from the base. Propagate them in a pot filled with sand and compost. Cover with clear plastic and place in a cold frame. Plant Madonna lilies.

06:50 — Tuesday **25**

◐ 17:57 — ♏ — Wednesday **26**

On August 27, do not garden between 06:50 and 16:50.
Blanch cardoon for 3–4 weeks, celery for 2–3 weeks and chicory for 10–15 days.

☋ 11:52 — 12:50 — Thursday **27**

14:03 — ♐ — Friday **28**

Harvest the first apples and pears, strawberries and climbing raspberries. Pick shelling beans (for drying), shell them and put the beans in the freezer for a few days to kill any broad bean beetles.

Ascending moon

Saturday **29** — 19:50

♑ — Sunday **30**

In mild regions, in the nursery, sow onions (*Long Red Florence, Spanish*) and white pickling onions (*Paris Silverskin, Barletta Silverskin, de Vaugirard*). A few days after they start to sprout, thin them to one plant every 5 cm (2 in).

Monday **31**

Your notes and observations

September 2020

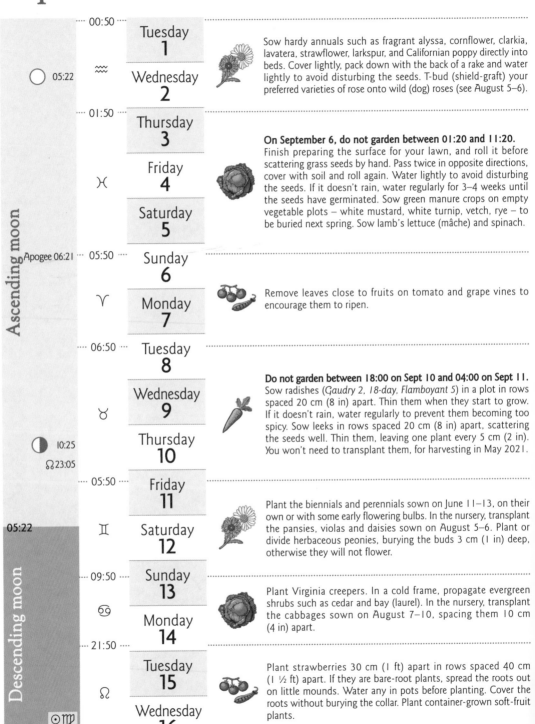

Ascending moon

○ 05:22 ♒

00:50

Tuesday 1

Wednesday 2

Sow hardy annuals such as fragrant alyssa, cornflower, clarkia, lavatera, strawflower, larkspur, and Californian poppy directly into beds. Cover lightly, pack down with the back of a rake and water lightly to avoid disturbing the seeds. T-bud (shield-graft) your preferred varieties of rose onto wild (dog) roses (see August 5–6).

01:50

Thursday 3

♓

Friday 4

Saturday 5

On September 6, do not garden between 01:20 and 11:20.
Finish preparing the surface for your lawn, and roll it before scattering grass seeds by hand. Pass twice in opposite directions, cover with soil and roll again. Water lightly to avoid disturbing the seeds. If it doesn't rain, water regularly for 3–4 weeks until the seeds have germinated. Sow green manure crops on empty vegetable plots – white mustard, white turnip, vetch, rye – to be buried next spring. Sow lamb's lettuce (mâche) and spinach.

Apogee 06:21 · 05:50

Sunday 6

♈

Monday 7

Remove leaves close to fruits on tomato and grape vines to encourage them to ripen.

06:50

Tuesday 8

♉

Wednesday 9

Thursday 10

Do not garden between 18:00 on Sept 10 and 04:00 on Sept 11.
Sow radishes (*Gaudry 2, 18-day, Flamboyant 5*) in a plot in rows spaced 20 cm (8 in) apart. Thin them when they start to grow. If it doesn't rain, water regularly to prevent them becoming too spicy. Sow leeks in rows spaced 20 cm (8 in) apart, scattering the seeds well. Thin them, leaving one plant every 5 cm (2 in). You won't need to transplant them, for harvesting in May 2021.

◑ 10:25
☊23:05

05:50

Friday 11

05:22

♊

Saturday 12

Plant the biennials and perennials sown on June 11–13, on their own or with some early flowering bulbs. In the nursery, transplant the pansies, violas and daisies sown on August 5–6. Plant or divide herbaceous peonies, burying the buds 3 cm (1 in) deep, otherwise they will not flower.

Descending moon

09:50

Sunday 13

♋

Monday 14

Plant Virginia creepers. In a cold frame, propagate evergreen shrubs such as cedar and bay (laurel). In the nursery, transplant the cabbages sown on August 7–10, spacing them 10 cm (4 in) apart.

21:50

Tuesday 15

♌

Wednesday 16

Plant strawberries 30 cm (1 ft) apart in rows spaced 40 cm (1 ½ ft) apart. If they are bare-root plants, spread the roots out on little mounds. Water any in pots before planting. Cover the roots without burying the collar. Plant container-grown soft-fruit plants.

⊙ ♍

Your notes and observations

September 2020

All times are displayed in GMT. In UK/Ireland add 1 hour for BST

Descending moon

☉ ♍ ♌

Wednesday 16

Place a flat stone under marrows and pumpkins to protect them from humidity and encourage them to ripen.

● 11:00 — 06:50

Thursday 17

Perigee 13:41 ♍

Friday 18

On September 18, do not garden between 08:40 and 18:40.
Start planting the onions sown on August 12–14. Move the strongest plants first, letting the others grow a little longer. Trim the tips of the leaves and the roots to 1 cm (½ in) from the bulb. Plant them in a sunny plot in rows spaced 15 cm (6 in) apart, with a plant every 8 cm (3 in), burying the bulbs 3 cm (1 in) deep. Pack down but do not water.

Saturday 19

07:50 — **Sunday 20**

♎

Plant shrubs that thrive in acid-rich soil such as azalea, rhododendron, kalmia and pieris, covering the soil with compost. Plant or divide lily of the valley in semi-shade. Space the plants 10 cm (4 in) apart. Plant container-grown perennials.

13:50 — **Monday 21**

Autumnal Equinox 13:30 ♏

Tuesday 22

On September 23, do not garden between 07:30 and 17:30.
Plant conifers, evergreen shrubs or deciduous hedges so they take root before the hard frosts. Blanch curly endive, escarole, cardoon and celery.

☋ 12:32 — 18:50

Wednesday 23

◗ 01:54
19:10 ♐

Thursday 24

In mild regions, sow round peas (*Petit Provençal, Douce Provence*) or mangetout (*Carouby de Maussane, Avalanche*). To provide graft stock, layer peach, apricot and plum pits in pots filled with sand and bury them at the foot of a north-facing wall. Harvest autumn apples and pears, grapes, strawberries and raspberries.

01:50 — **Friday 25**

Ascending moon

Saturday 26

♑

Under shelter, in well refined soil, sow medium-long carrots (*Touchon, Nandor, Bolero*) for harvesting in April–May 2021. Sift mature compost and spread it over vegetable plots or flowerbeds. Feed the new compost heap with seasonal waste.

Sunday 27

06:50 — **Monday 28**

♒

Sow perennial sweet peas in front of a trellis or wire fence. Dig little holes 3 cm (1 in) deep every 40 cm (1 ½ ft) and plant 4–5 seeds in each hole. Cover, pack down with your hands and water lightly. Mark where you planted them, as they won't germinate until next spring. Harvest saffron and leave it to dry.

Tuesday 29

07:50 — **Wednesday 30**

♓

Your notes and observations

September

October 2020

Ascending moon

○ 21:05

H

Apogee 18:08 ···· 12:50 ····

Υ

···· 13:40 ····

℧

☊ 00:29 ···· 12:50 ····

II

13:05
◑ 00:39

···· 17:50 ····

Descending moon

♋

···· 07:50 ····

♌

···· 17:50 ····

♍

19:31
Perigee 23:40

Thursday 1

Friday 2

Saturday 3

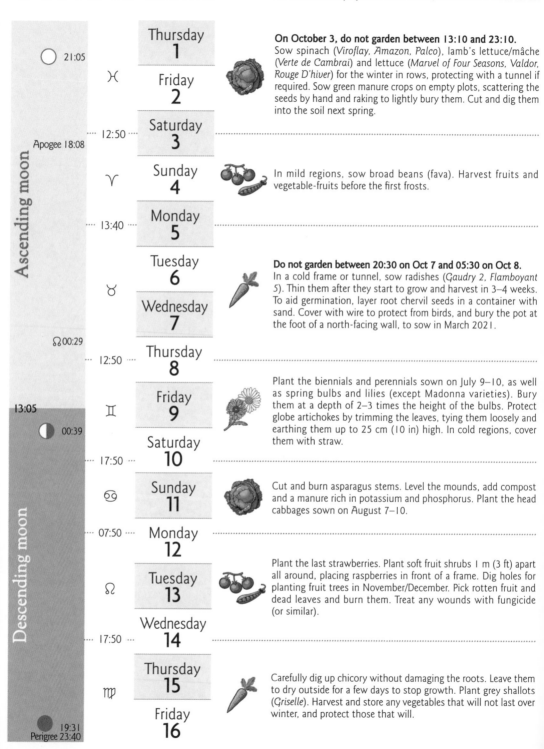

On October 3, do not garden between 13:10 and 23:10.
Sow spinach (*Viroflay, Amazon, Palco*), lamb's lettuce/mâche (*Verte de Cambrai*) and lettuce (*Marvel of Four Seasons, Valdor, Rouge D'hiver*) for the winter in rows, protecting with a tunnel if required. Sow green manure crops on empty plots, scattering the seeds by hand and raking to lightly bury them. Cut and dig them into the soil next spring.

Sunday 4

In mild regions, sow broad beans (fava). Harvest fruits and vegetable-fruits before the first frosts.

Monday 5

Tuesday 6

Wednesday 7

Do not garden between 20:30 on Oct 7 and 05:30 on Oct 8.
In a cold frame or tunnel, sow radishes (*Gaudry 2, Flamboyant 5*). Thin them after they start to grow and harvest in 3–4 weeks. To aid germination, layer root chervil seeds in a container with sand. Cover with wire to protect from birds, and bury the pot at the foot of a north-facing wall, to sow in March 2021.

Thursday 8

Friday 9

Plant the biennials and perennials sown on July 9–10, as well as spring bulbs and lilies (except Madonna varieties). Bury them at a depth of 2–3 times the height of the bulbs. Protect globe artichokes by trimming the leaves, tying them loosely and earthing them up to 25 cm (10 in) high. In cold regions, cover them with straw.

Saturday 10

Sunday 11

Cut and burn asparagus stems. Level the mounds, add compost and a manure rich in potassium and phosphorus. Plant the head cabbages sown on August 7–10.

Monday 12

Tuesday 13

Plant the last strawberries. Plant soft fruit shrubs 1 m (3 ft) apart all around, placing raspberries in front of a frame. Dig holes for planting fruit trees in November/December. Pick rotten fruit and dead leaves and burn them. Treat any wounds with fungicide (or similar).

Wednesday 14

Thursday 15

Carefully dig up chicory without damaging the roots. Leave them to dry outside for a few days to stop growth. Plant grey shallots (*Griselle*). Harvest and store any vegetables that will not last over winter, and protect those that will.

Friday 16

Your notes and observations

October

October 2020

All times are displayed in GMT. In UK/Ireland add 1 hour for BST

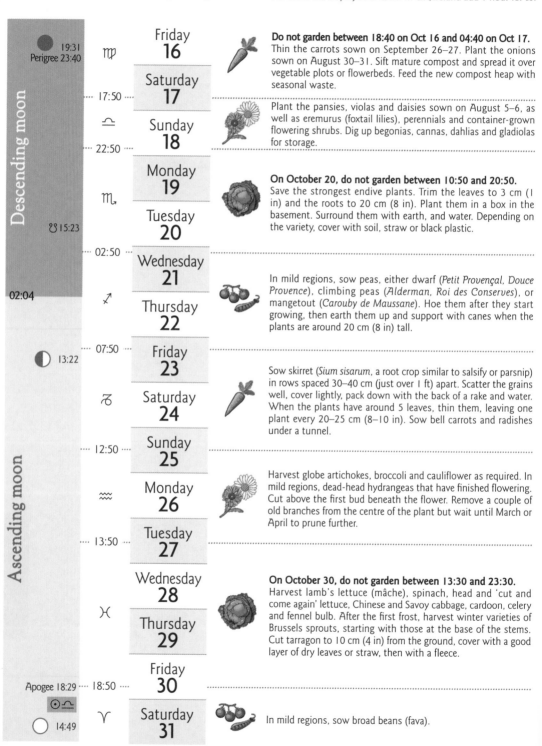

Descending moon

Friday 16 — 19:31 ● Perigree 23:40 — ♍

Do not garden between 18:40 on Oct 16 and 04:40 on Oct 17. Thin the carrots sown on September 26–27. Plant the onions sown on August 30–31. Sift mature compost and spread it over vegetable plots or flowerbeds. Feed the new compost heap with seasonal waste.

Saturday 17 — 17:50

Sunday 18 — ♎ ···· 22:50 ····

Plant the pansies, violas and daisies sown on August 5–6, as well as eremurus (foxtail lilies), perennials and container-grown flowering shrubs. Dig up begonias, cannas, dahlias and gladiolas for storage.

Monday 19 — ♏

Tuesday 20 — ☊ 15:23

On October 20, do not garden between 10:50 and 20:50. Save the strongest endive plants. Trim the leaves to 3 cm (1 in) and the roots to 20 cm (8 in). Plant them in a box in the basement. Surround them with earth, and water. Depending on the variety, cover with soil, straw or black plastic.

Wednesday 21 — 02:50

02:04

Thursday 22 — ♐

In mild regions, sow peas, either dwarf (*Petit Provençal, Douce Provence*), climbing peas (*Alderman, Roi des Conserves*), or mangetout (*Carouby de Maussane*). Hoe them after they start growing, then earth them up and support with canes when the plants are around 20 cm (8 in) tall.

Ascending moon

Friday 23 — ◑ 13:22 ···· 07:50 ····

Saturday 24 — ♑

Sow skirret (*Sium sisarum*, a root crop similar to salsify or parsnip) in rows spaced 30–40 cm (just over 1 ft) apart. Scatter the grains well, cover lightly, pack down with the back of a rake and water. When the plants have around 5 leaves, thin them, leaving one plant every 20–25 cm (8–10 in). Sow bell carrots and radishes under a tunnel.

Sunday 25 — 12:50

Monday 26 — ♒

Harvest globe artichokes, broccoli and cauliflower as required. In mild regions, dead-head hydrangeas that have finished flowering. Cut above the first bud beneath the flower. Remove a couple of old branches from the centre of the plant but wait until March or April to prune further.

Tuesday 27 — 13:50

Wednesday 28 — ♓

Thursday 29

On October 30, do not garden between 13:30 and 23:30. Harvest lamb's lettuce (mâche), spinach, head and 'cut and come again' lettuce, Chinese and Savoy cabbage, cardoon, celery and fennel bulb. After the first frost, harvest winter varieties of Brussels sprouts, starting with those at the base of the stems. Cut tarragon to 10 cm (4 in) from the ground, cover with a good layer of dry leaves or straw, then with a fleece.

Friday 30 — Apogee 18:29 ···· 18:50 ····

Saturday 31 — ⊙♎ — ○ 14:49 — ♈

In mild regions, sow broad beans (fava).

Your notes and observations

November 2020

All times are displayed in GMT using the 24-hour clock

Ascending moon

Ω 02:39

18:50

Υ — Sunday **1**

Harvest fruit such as medlars and persimmons (Sharon fruit). If it's not too cold, spread them out on crates on a bed of straw. Eat them overripe.

Monday **2**

Ö — Tuesday **3**

Do not garden between 21:40 on Nov 3 and 07:40 on Nov 4. Make use of this quiet gardening period to take stock of your crops over the past year and note areas for improvement. Start planning your vegetable garden for 2021. Consider crop rotation – don't grow the same vegetable in the same plot for 3–5 years – and plant companionships (see p. 28–29). Identify any plots that shouldn't be fertilised.

18:50

Wednesday **4**

19:30

Ⅱ — Thursday **5**

After the first frosts, pull up tuberous begonias, dahlias, cannas and gladiolas, and store them in a dry, frost-free place. Dig up and dispose of annuals. Plant a clematis with support, hemerocallis (daylilies) and bare-root peonies.

Friday **6**

00:50

Saturday **7**

♋ — Sunday **8**

Blanch endive, cardoon and celery. Clean dandelions and cover them with opaque pots for harvesting in 3–4 weeks.

13:46

15:50

Descending moon

Monday **9**

Ω — Tuesday **10**

If there's no frost, plant bare-root fruit trees and vines, keeping the grafting sites above ground. Support with stakes, and water copiously. When the fruit trees shed their leaves, spray them with fungicide (or similar). Take cuttings of fig tree branches. Bury them at the foot of a north-facing wall, leaving the ends just poking out. Earth up the beans sown on October 4.

03:50

Wednesday **11**

Thursday **12**

♍ — Friday **13**

Pull up Jerusalem and Chinese artichokes, salsify, horseradish, parsnips and leeks as required. Spread a layer of straw over the soil to protect crops from the frost and continue your harvest. In mild regions, plant shallots (*Jermor, Longor, Mikor*) and grey shallots (*Griselle*), barely burying the pointy tips. Plant white and purple garlic. Dig heavy soil in big clods without damaging roots.

Perigee 11:36

06:50

Saturday **14**

♎

05:07

10:50

On November 14, do not garden between 06:40 and 16:40. Cut back dried growth on perennials. Crush and compost the waste if it's healthy. Don't cut back grass or non-hardy plants. Prune rose shrubs and treat with fungicide (or similar).

Sunday **15**

♏ — Monday **16**

Force endives (see p.21), cutting the leaves to 1 cm (½ in) and the roots to 20 cm (8 in). Plant the roots in a ditch in the garden or box in the basement.

Your notes and observations

November 2020

All times are displayed in GMT using the 24-hour clock

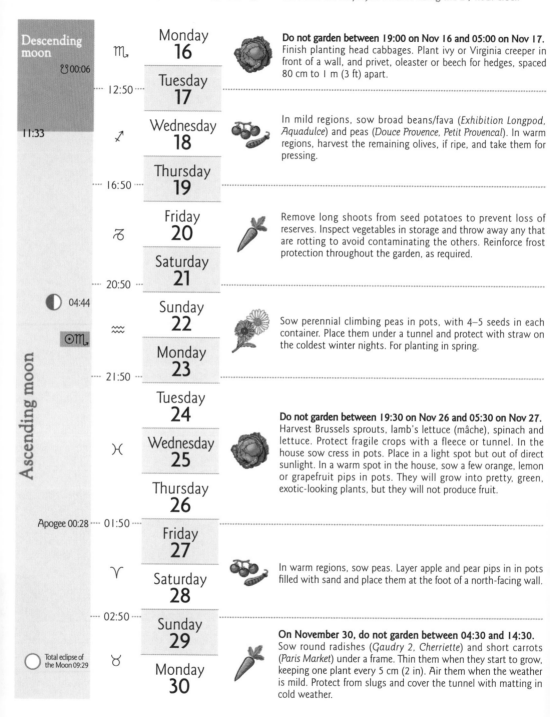

Descending moon

☊ 00:06

11:33

--- 12:50

♏

Monday 16

Tuesday 17

Do not garden between 19:00 on Nov 16 and 05:00 on Nov 17. Finish planting head cabbages. Plant ivy or Virginia creeper in front of a wall, and privet, oleaster or beech for hedges, spaced 80 cm to 1 m (3 ft) apart.

♐

Wednesday 18

--- 16:50

Thursday 19

In mild regions, sow broad beans/fava (*Exhibition Longpod, Aquadulce*) and peas (*Douce Provence, Petit Provençal*). In warm regions, harvest the remaining olives, if ripe, and take them for pressing.

♑

Friday 20

Saturday 21

Remove long shoots from seed potatoes to prevent loss of reserves. Inspect vegetables in storage and throw away any that are rotting to avoid contaminating the others. Reinforce frost protection throughout the garden, as required.

--- 20:50

◐ 04:44

o♏

≈

Sunday 22

Monday 23

Sow perennial climbing peas in pots, with 4–5 seeds in each container. Place them under a tunnel and protect with straw on the coldest winter nights. For planting in spring.

--- 21:50

Ascending moon

Tuesday 24

♓

Wednesday 25

Do not garden between 19:30 on Nov 26 and 05:30 on Nov 27. Harvest Brussels sprouts, lamb's lettuce (mâche), spinach and lettuce. Protect fragile crops with a fleece or tunnel. In the house sow cress in pots. Place in a light spot but out of direct sunlight. In a warm spot in the house, sow a few orange, lemon or grapefruit pips in pots. They will grow into pretty, green, exotic-looking plants, but they will not produce fruit.

Thursday 26

Apogee 00:28 --- 01:50

♈

Friday 27

Saturday 28

In warm regions, sow peas. Layer apple and pear pips in in pots filled with sand and place them at the foot of a north-facing wall.

--- 02:50

○ Total eclipse of the Moon 09:29

♉

Sunday 29

Monday 30

On November 30, do not garden between 04:30 and 14:30. Sow round radishes (*Gaudry 2, Cherriette*) and short carrots (*Paris Market*) under a frame. Thin them when they start to grow, keeping one plant every 5 cm (2 in). Air them when the weather is mild. Protect from slugs and cover the tunnel with matting in cold weather.

Your notes and observations

December 2020

Ascending moon ☊07:45

00:41

Descending moon

01:50

♉

♊

07:50

♋

21:50

♌

01:36

11:50

♍

16:50

♎

Perigee 20:34

21:50

♏

☋11:02
Total eclipse of the Sun 16:16

23:50

22:24
Ascending moon ♐

Tuesday **1**	**On December 1, do not garden between 02:45 and 12:45.** Stratify root chervil seeds in a pot filled with sand.
Wednesday **2**	If there is no frost, plant roses and bare-root shrubs. Work compost into the roots to help them take well, and enrich the soil with horn meal and compost. Earth up the grafting sites of newly planted or non-hardy roses until spring. Take cuttings from and plant wild (dog) roses for grafting next summer.
Thursday **3**	
Friday **4**	Force more endives, in the garden or the basement. Blanch dandelions. If the ground isn't frozen, plant a hedge of deciduous shrubs. Dig holes and enrich the soil with compost. Remove the shrubs from their pots, plant, fill the holes, pack down and water. Prune hazel branches.
Saturday **5**	
Sunday **6**	When it's not frosty, plant container-grown or bare-root fruit trees. Prune any bushy pip-fruit varieties. Remove excess growth and a few old or less productive branches to let in air and light. Brush the trunks to remove moss and lichens, and burn the waste. Transplant excess raspberry shoots.
Monday **7**	
Tuesday **8**	
Wednesday **9**	Keep digging heavy soil, without breaking up clods, for refining and levelling in spring. In mild regions, plant white and purple garlic in a plot that has not been manured recently. Harvest Chinese artichokes, parsnips, Jerusalem artichokes and salsify as required. Conserve some good artichoke and horseradish tubers to restart the crop next spring.
Thursday **10**	
Friday **11**	**On December 12, do not garden between 15:30 and 24:00.** In milder weather, air globe artichokes; in colder weather, check frost protection throughout the garden. Indoors, plant amaryllis in pots. Bury the bulbs to half their height in a light compost, leaving the top part uncovered.
Saturday **12**	
Sunday **13**	**On December 14, do not garden between 06:00 and 21:15.** On a mild day, prune deciduous trees, keeping a good shape. Remove dead wood to air the remaining branches. Remove any mistletoe and branches with burrs. Apply mastic (or similar) to wounds.
Monday **14**	
Tuesday **15**	If it isn't frosty, take cuttings from fruit trees for grafting in the spring. Cut healthy twigs with strong buds to lengths of 30 cm (1 ft). Tie them in bundles, label them and half-bury them at the foot of an east or north-facing wall.
Wednesday **16**	

Your notes and observations

December 2020

Wednesday 16 ♐

In mild regions, sow broad beans/fava (*Exhibition Longpod, Aquadulce*) 5 cm (2 in) deep.

···· 02:50

☉♐

Thursday 17 ♑

Friday 18

When you have decided on your plan for next year's garden, determine which seeds you need and buy them. Clean tools, sand wooden handles and oil them. Sharpen and grease spade blades.

···· 05:50

Saturday 19

♒

Sunday 20

In a warm place, sow begonia semperflorens and pelargoniums in pots. Make little furrows and scatter the seeds well. Don't cover them, simply pack down with a board. Graft the campsis grown in pots. Keep them in the greenhouse, for planting in spring with a firm support.

Winter Solstice 10:02
···· 04:50

Monday 21

◗ 23:41

Tuesday 22 ♓

Wednesday 23

On December 24, do not garden between 11:30 and 21:30.
If there's no frost, harvest Brussels sprouts, head and Savoy cabbages, lamb's lettuce (mâche) and spinach. Indoors, sprout lentils, chickpeas and soybeans in little dishes. Their young shoots are packed with vitamins and minerals. Sow golden purslane in pots, scattering the seeds well. Cover lightly, pack down with a board and humidify.

···· 08:50

Apogee 16:26

Thursday 24

♈

Friday 25

In mild regions, sow broad beans (fava) and dwarf or climbing peas.

···· 09:50

Saturday 26

Sunday 27

♉

Monday 28

On December 28, do not garden between 10:00 and 20:00.
Sow radishes (*Gaudry 2, Cherriette, Flamboyant 5*) and short carrots (Paris Market) in a cold frame. Mix the two seeds; when you harvest the radishes, thin the carrots. Cover lightly, pack down with a board and water lightly. Air them in the middle of the day when the weather is mild. Protect from slugs and from the cold, with matting, if required.

☊ 15:02

···· 08:50

Tuesday 29

○ 03:28

07:54

Wednesday 30 ♊

When there's no frost, plant roses, shrubs and flowering climbers. Coat bare roots with compost or hydrate the clods before removing from pots. Dig large holes to loosen the soil, and mix in horn meal and compost. Plant, with support for climbing plants. Fill in holes, pack down and water.

Descending moon

···· 13:50

Thursday 31 ♋

Happy New Year!

Ascending moon

Your notes and observations

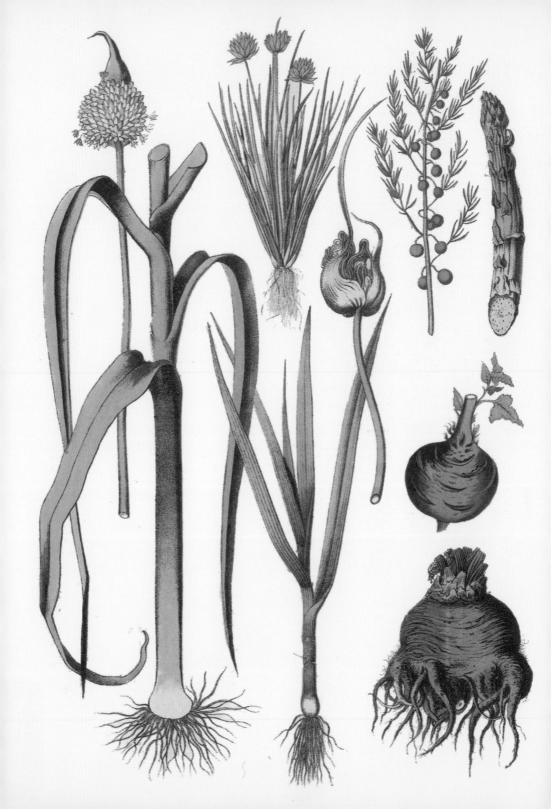

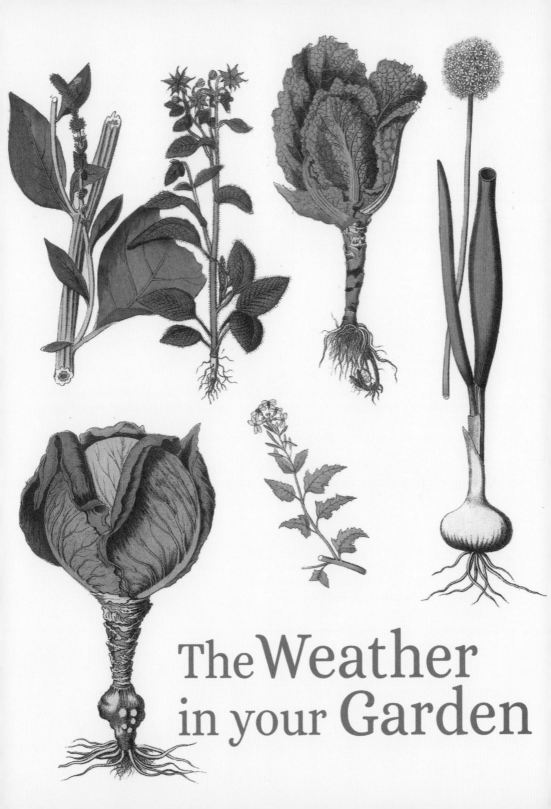

The Weather
in your Garden

Your Weather Journal

Observing the weather

You will often notice differences between the weather forecast and the actual weather in your garden. There are several ways to better predict the weather where you live, but here we will look at the simplest and most natural.

It also helps to record details about the weather in a logbook and on the monthly charts provided here (pp. 92–103). The more specific your notes are, the more accurate your predictions will become. In turn, you will take greater pleasure in observing nature and the movements of the sky. A logbook is a very useful tool for recording your gardening experience. You can carry it over from year to year, enriching your knowledge and easing the planning of seasonal and daily tasks.

What to look for

Altitude and other features of the local landscape can affect the weather in your garden: there may be a hill or mountain nearby, or perhaps a tree, hedge or wall protects you from the wind. The reverse may be true: a valley might channel important air currents, or a nearby lake may create an updraught. Microclimates are infinite and your garden is unique, which means so are its weather patterns.

Will it be warm and sunny? Will it rain? It can help to look at the sky for clues. A bright moon surrounded by a halo, or a veiled sun in the evening often mean rain.

Through observation, you can learn which wind drives away clouds, clears the sky or allows the Sun to shine. Birds and insects can 'smell' the rain or an approaching thunderstorm, behaving in ways we can recognise and use too. The shape of the clouds can also help; consult an illustrated book on clouds for reference.

Soli-lunar charts

How to use them

The soli-lunar charts shown here are graduated in 5° bands with 0° marking the equator. Positive declinations are above the equator line and negative declinations below. If you are in the Southern hemisphere, turn the chart upside down.

- Dates of the lunar phases, Moon nodes, perigees and apogees are all marked and a key to symbols used is provided on p.36
- The path of the Sun is marked in dark green, and the Moon in light green
- As in the example on p.90, make notes every day, for example the colour of the sky, any rain, sun, clear weather, variable wind, the lowest night temperature, highest daytime temperature, etc.

The Sun

On January 1 at midnight (00:00), the declination[1] of the Sun is −23°03′ (see chart p. 92). The Sun is gaining height from its lowest point at the winter solstice.

At the time of the spring equinox, the curve of the Sun intersects with the equator and day and night are the same duration. The Sun's declination becomes positive, temperatures gradually climb, sap rises in plants and flowers start to bloom.

The Sun reaches its highest point (+23°26′) at the time of the summer solstice on June 20, before starting its descent, crossing the equator again at the time of the autumn equinox (p. 100) and falling to its lowest level at the winter solstice (23°26′, p. 103).

The constant pace of the Sun, identical every year, regulates the length of our days, and the rise and fall of plants' sap.

The Moon

The Moon's movement changes from one year to the next in relation to the Earth, the Sun and the ecliptic, thus causing many variations.

At the start of 2020 the Moon is ascending, arriving at its highest lunistice when in Gemini on January 10 at 6:00. It then descends, crossing the celestial equator on January 16, to reach its lowest lunistice[2] on January 23 at 4:00 in Sagittarius.

There are 13 days, 15 hours, 15 minutes and 30 seconds between two lunistices and the crossings of the equator, the complete cycle of the sidereal revolution being 27 days, 7 hours, 43 minutes and 11 seconds.

Changes in weather usually occur at the time of lunistices, especially on the third day.

Let's take an example in April

Note carefully the weather on April 1, 2, and 3 in particular.

- If the weather is fair and the wind blows from the direction of the good weather, it should last until the full moon on the 8th.
- If the weather is variable on the 3rd, changeable with cloudy skies and rain showers, you can expect sunny intervals ahead. Note that on the day the Moon crosses the equator (7th) there may be some small changes.

Remember, when it comes to weather forecasting, no system is infallible. Hopefully, this method will help you to plan your gardening tasks in some way.

---

1 Declination: distance of a star from the plane of the celestial equator (horizontal line 0° on the charts).
2 Lunistice: time when the Moon reaches the farthest distance north or south of the celestial equator.

Soli-lunar Charts

How to use the charts: an example

Each monthly chart allows you to note the main weather variations each day.

	Rain (mm) daily	month to date	Temperature (°C) min	max	Wind	Air pressure	Weather features
31 Tue			5	10	SE		Fair sunny intervals, mild
30 Mon	3	62	4	7		1042	Overcast, drizzle, mild
29 Sun			−2	7		1045	Fog, rain, sunny intervals
28 Sat	10	59	2	6		1040	Light showers, fog in the evening
27 Fri			5	3	SE	1036	Cloudy
26 Thu			−6	2	SE	1036	Overcast, wind gusts in the evening
25 Wed			−8	4		1042	Sunny intervals
24 Tue			−8	4	N	1043	Fair
23 Mon			−3	6		1042	Fair to cloudy
22 Sun Ap.			−4	7		1044	Overcast
21 Sat			−6	8		1045	Fair
20 Fri			−7	3		1046	Fair
19 Thu			−11	3		1046	Fair, milder
18 Wed			−11	−1		1045	Sunny, cold
17 Tue			−7	1	NE	1041	Fair, cold
16 Mon	2	49	−2	2	N	1042	Some snow in the morning, sunny intervals
15 Sun	3	47	−3	1		1043	Snow in the morning, some sun
14 Sat	22	44	−4	1		1042	Snow turning to rain
13 Fri	4	22	−1	5		1039	Snow early and for the rest of the day
12 Thu	5	18	2	6		1032	Fog, rain
11 Wed	13		−2	5		1045	Fog, rain
10 Tue Pér.			1	5	NO	1036	Fog, overcast
9 Mon			−6	3		1044	Sunny intervals
8 Sun			−4	4		1050	Fair
7 Sat			−7	5		1051	Fair
6 Fri			−8	1		1053	Fair, some clouds
5 Thu			−4	3	NO	1051	Fair
4 Wed			−8	2		1045	Fair, milder
3 Tue			−6	3	NO	1047	Fair, then cold
2 Mon			−5	5		1045	Sunny intervals, light clouds
1 Sun			−3	5		1044	Fair

+30° +25° +20° +15° +10° +5° 0° −5° −10° −15° −20° −25° −30°

This example was noted in January 2017. The third day after the lunistice, January 13 and 27 provide important indications for the 10 days following.

In dark green, the passage of the Sun in front of Sagittarius and Capricorn. In light green, the curve and passage of the Moon in front of the constellations.

90

This chart allows you to visualise the large curve of the Sun, the small monthly curves of the Moon, their ascending movement (times for sowing) and descending movement (times for preparing the earth, transplanting and planting).

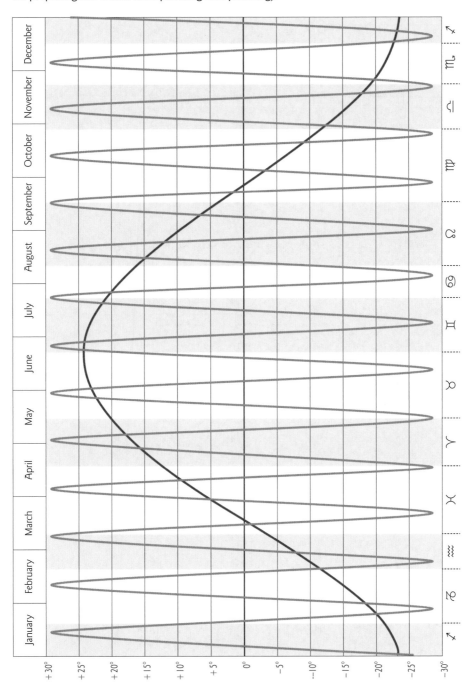

January 2020

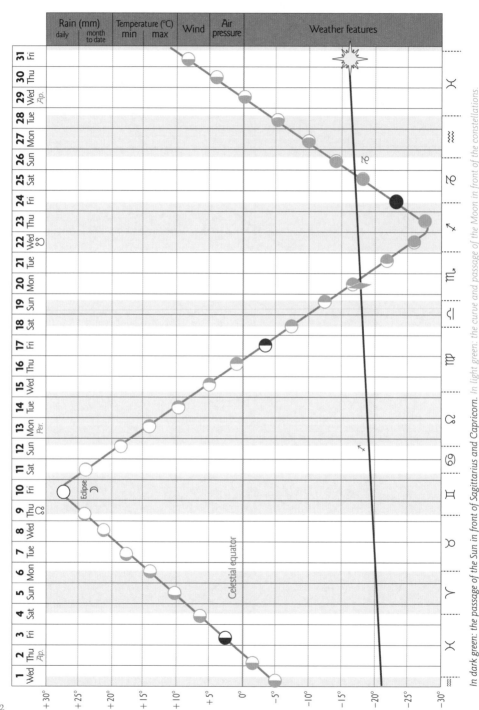

| Rain (mm) | | Temperature (°C) | | Wind | Air pressure | Weather features |
| daily | month to date | min | max | | | |

In dark green: the passage of the Sun in front of Sagittarius and Capricorn. In light green: the curve and passage of the Moon in front of the constellations.

February 2020

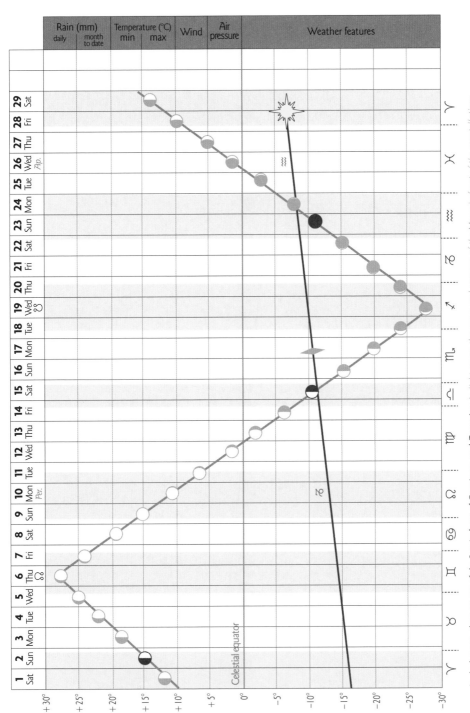

	Rain (mm)		Temperature (°C)		Wind	Air pressure	Weather features
	daily	month to date	min	max			

In dark green: the passage of the Sun in front of Capricorn and Aquarius. In light green: the curve and passage of the Moon in front of the constellations.

March 2020

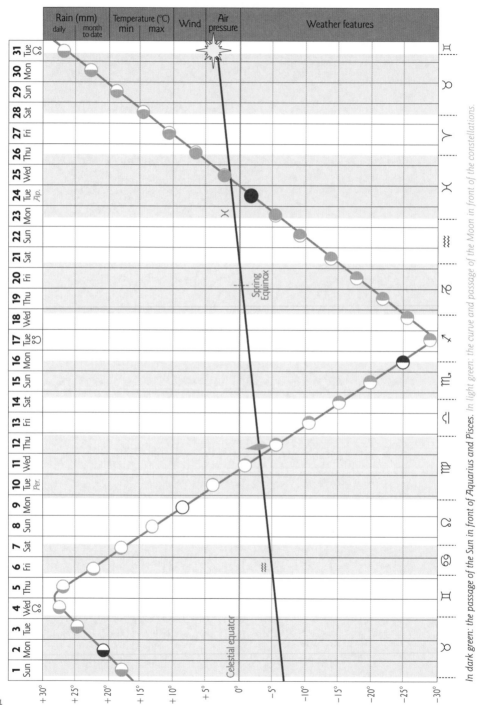

	Rain (mm)		Temperature (°C)		Wind	Air pressure	Weather features
	daily	month to date	min	max			

In dark green: the passage of the Sun in front of Aquarius and Pisces. In light green: the curve and passage of the Moon in front of the constellations.

94

April 2020

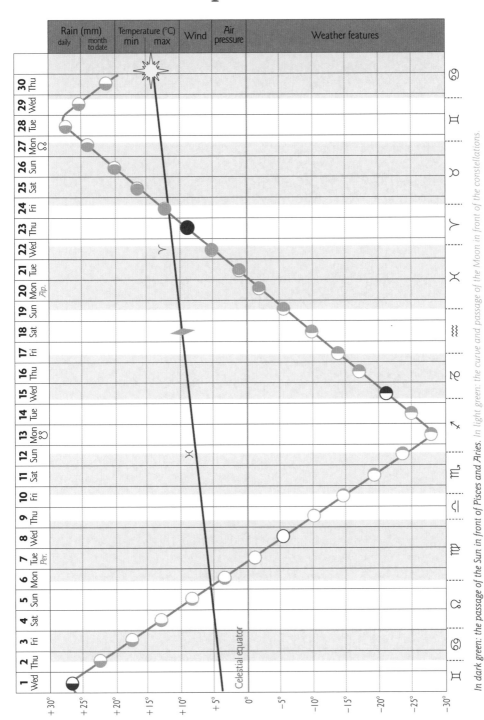

| | Rain (mm) | | Temperature (°C) | | Wind | Air pressure | Weather features |
| | daily | month to date | min | max | | | |

May 2020

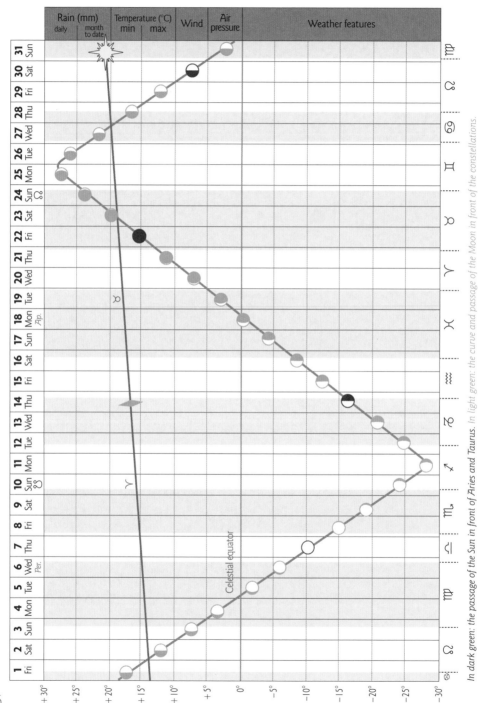

In dark green: the passage of the Sun in front of Aries and Taurus. In light green: the curve and passage of the Moon in front of the constellations.

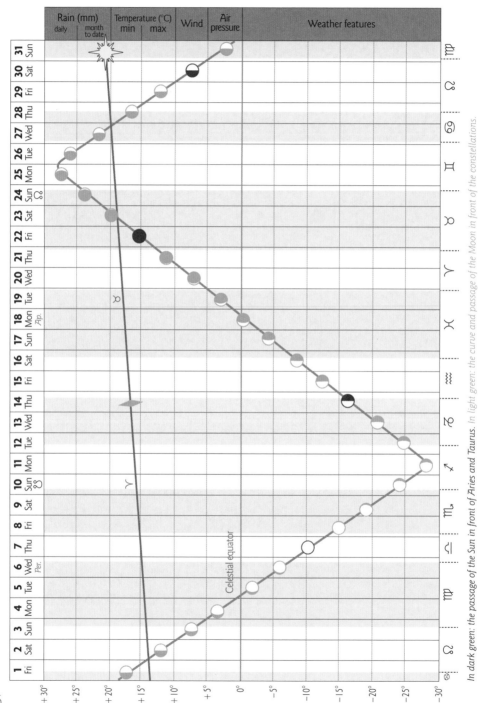

June 2020

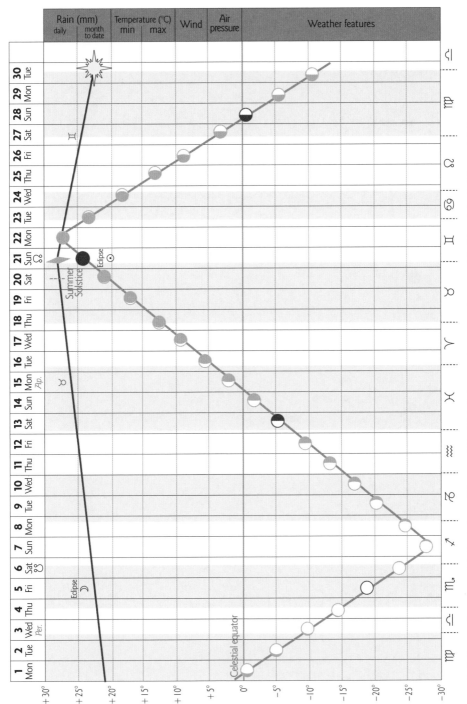

In dark green: the passage of the Sun in front of Taurus and Gemini. In light green: the curve and passage of the Moon in front of the constellations.

July 2020

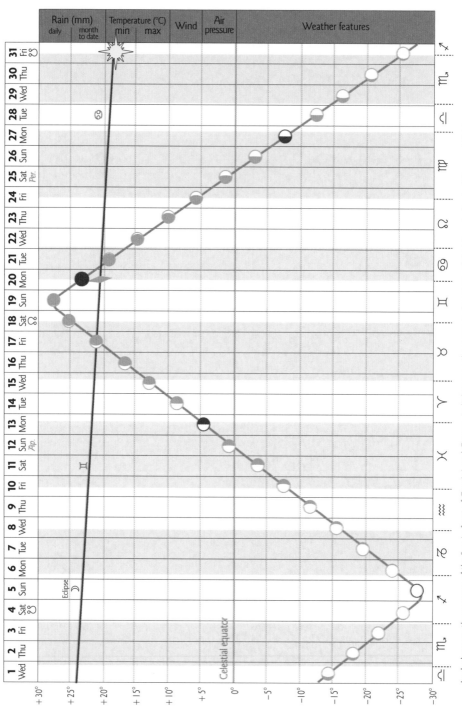

In dark green: the passage of the Sun in front of Gemini and Cancer. In light green: the curve and passage of the Moon in front of the constellations.

August 2020

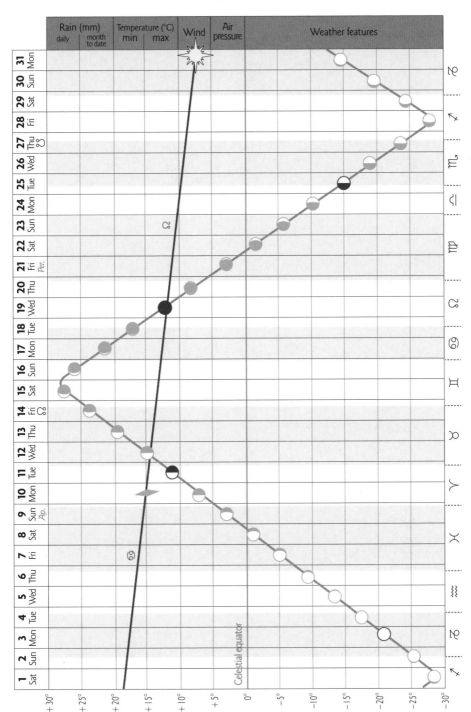

		Rain (mm)		Temperature (°C)		Wind	Air pressure	Weather features
		daily	month to date	min	max			

In dark green: the passage of the Sun in front of Cancer and Leo. In light green: the curve and passage of the Moon in front of the constellations.

September 2020

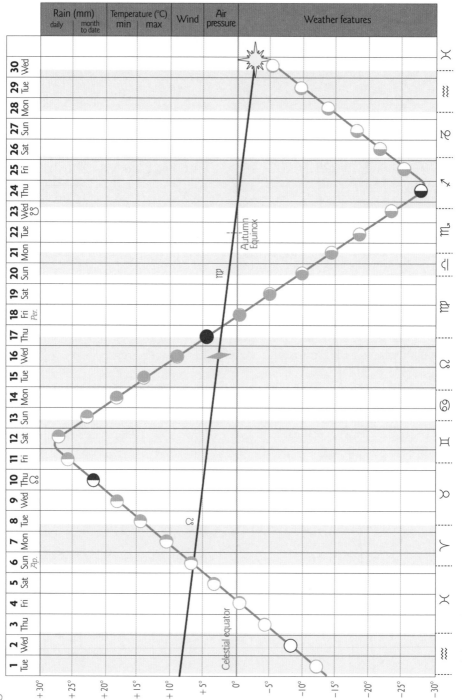

Rain (mm)		Temperature (°C)		Wind	Air pressure	Weather features
daily	month to date	min	max			

In dark green: the passage of the Sun in front of Leo and Virgo. In light green: the curve and passage of the Moon in front of the constellations.

October 2020

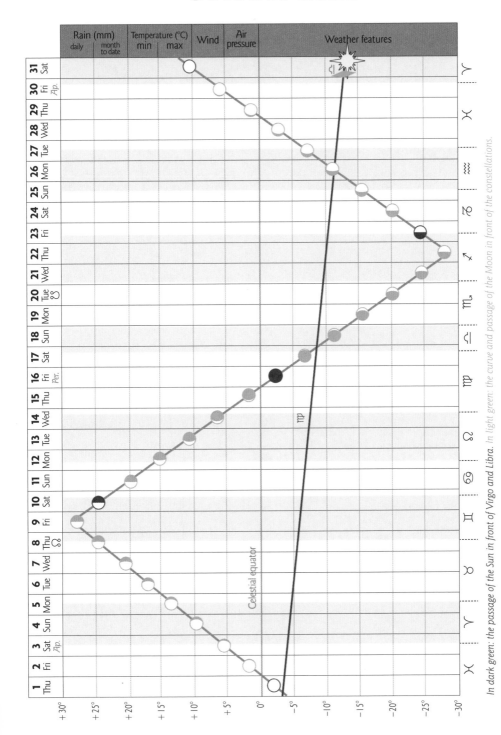

In dark green: the passage of the Sun in front of Virgo and Libra. In light green: the curve and passage of the Moon in front of the constellations.

November 2020

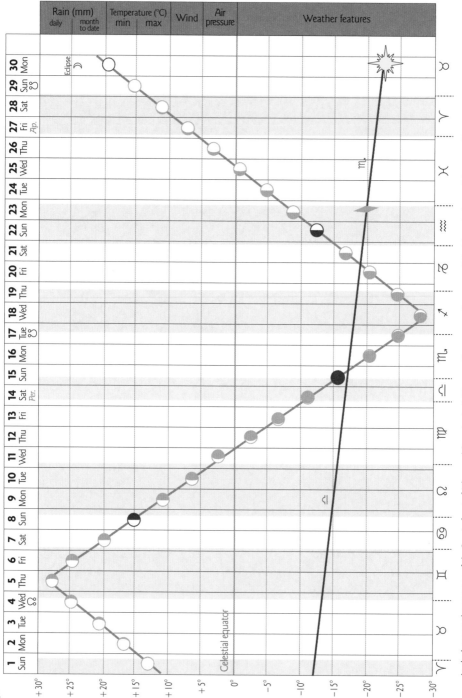

| Rain (mm) | | Temperature (°C) | | Wind | Air pressure | Weather features |
| daily | month to date | min | max | | | |

In dark green: the passage of the Sun in front of Libra and Scorpio. In light green: the curve and passage of the Moon in front of the constellations.

December 2020

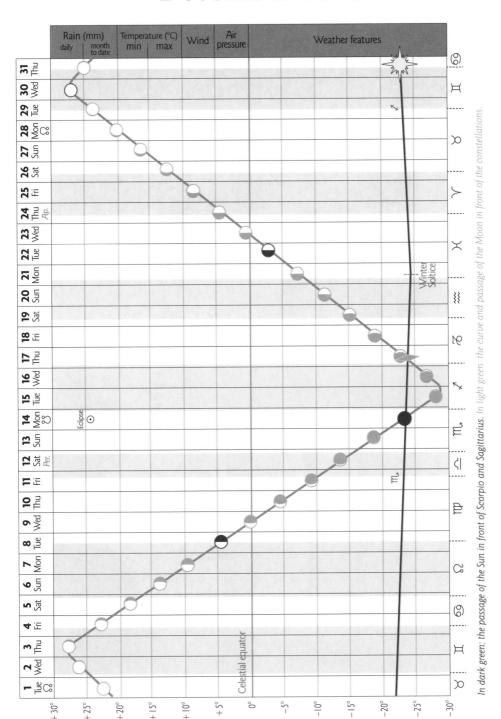

In dark green: the passage of the Sun in front of Scorpio and Sagittarius. In light green: the curve and passage of the Moon in front of the constellations.

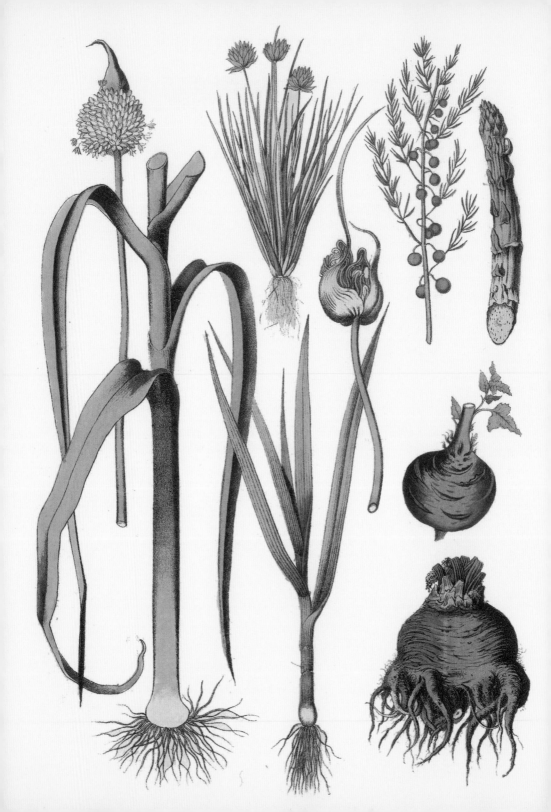

Crop
Tables

Annual crop tables

These annual crop tables will give you the best dates for sowing, planting and pruning according to the Moon. It is up to you to decide your personal gardening methods, and whether to grow your crops somewhere sheltered or on open ground, depending on the climate of your garden. The calendar pages (pp. 38–85) give all the necessary details about the Moon's cycles, but you can use them with the crop tables to keep track of which tasks you should do on a particular day by looking for the highlighted dates. Suggested soil temperatures stated on the tables are for sowing in the open earth (unless otherwise specified), but note that soil temperatures need to be higher for early seeding in containers. As mentioned earlier, it may be that you can't always follow our indicated harvest dates. On these days, we would suggest you make use of time indoors and do some garden planning, or perhaps make preserves with any crops you have already grown and harvested.

In the Vegetable Garden

Flowering vegetables

- Sow and plant in the greenhouse, under cover or in the open, depending on the season and the climate of your garden
- Sow with the ascendant Moon in Aquarius ♒
- Plant, hoe and earth up with the descending Moon in Gemini ♊ or Libra ♎

	Jan	Feb	Mar	Apr	May	Jun	Jul	Aug	Sep	Oct	Nov	Dec
Artichoke (globe)												
→ Remove cover. Keep two suckers from each stem		7/15	5/13	2/10/29				16/24	12/20	26		
→ Plant			5/13	2/10/29				16/24	12/20	10/18		
→ Water, fertilise, hoe			5/13	2/10/29	7/26	4/22/30	1/20/28	16/24	12/20			
→ Harvest					15	11	9	5	1/29			
→ Tie down, cover										10/18	6/15	3/12
Broccoli												
→ Sow (soil at 15 °C/60 °F*)		23	21	18	15	11	9					
→ Water lightly, transplant, hoe			13	2/10/29	7/26	4/22/30	1/20/28	16/24	12/20	10/18		
→ Harvest						11	9	5	1/29	26	22	
Cauliflower												
→ Sow (soil at 15 °C/60 °F*)	1/27	23	21	18	15	11						
→ Water regularly, transplant, hoe		7/15	5/13	2/10/29	7/26	4/22/30	1/20/28	16/24	12/20	10/18		
→ Harvest			21	18	15	11	9	5	1/29	26	22	19

The cultivation of the vegetable is explained in the Calendar on the highlighted date.

*Ideal soil temperature for good germination.

Leafy vegetables

- Sow and plant in the greenhouse, under cover or in the open depending on the season and the climate of your garden
- Sow with the ascendant Moon in Pisces ♓
- Plant, hoe and earth up with the descending Moon in Cancer ♋ or Scorpio ♏

	Jan	Feb	Mar	Apr	May	Jun	Jul	Aug	Sep	Oct	Nov	Dec
Asparagus												
☞ Prepare and enrich the soil	12/20	8/17								11/19	7/16	
☞ Plant 1–2 year-old crowns			6/15	3/11/30								
☞ Hoe, earth up			6/15	3/11/30								
☞ Harvest the older plants				21	19							
☞ Cut back, burn, add compost										11/19	7/16	
Cardoon												
☞ Prepare and enrich the soil			6/15	3/11/30						11/19	7/16	
☞ Sow (soil at 10 °C/50 °F*)					19							
☞ Thin plants, hoe, water						5/24	3/21/30	17/26	14/22			
☞ Earth up, blanch								17/26	14/22	11/19	7/16	
☞ Harvest									4	1/28	25	22
Celery												
☞ Prepare and enrich the soil		8/17	6/15									
☞ Sow (soil at 12 °C/53 °F*)			25	21	19							
☞ Transplant, plant, hoe				3/11/30	9/27	5/24	3/21/30	17/26	14/22			
☞ Earth up, blanch							3/21/30	17/26	14/22	11/19	7/16	
☞ Harvest								8	4	1/28	25	22
Chicory (witloof/endive)												
☞ Transplant, force, blanch	12/20	8/17								11/19	7/16	5/13
Fennel												
☞ Prepare and enrich the soil			6/15									
☞ Sow (soil at 12 °C/53 °F*)				21	19	14	11	8				
☞ Thin out, plant, earth up					9/27	5/24	3/21/30	17/26	14/22	11/19		
☞ Harvest							11	8	4	1/28	25	22
Spinach												
☞ Prepare and enrich the soil	12/20	8/17					3/21/30	17/26	14/22	11/19	7/16	
☞ Sow (soil at 12 °C/53 °F*)		1/26	25	21				8	4	1		
☞ Thin out, hoe		17	6/15	3/11/30	9			26	14/22	11/19	7/16	
☞ Harvest	2/29	1/26	25	21	19					1/28	25	22
Swiss chard												
☞ Prepare and enrich the soil			6/15							11/19	7/16	
☞ Sow (soil at 10 °C/50 °F*)				21	19	14						
☞ Thin, hoe					9/27	5/24	3/21/30	17/26	14/22	11/19		
☞ Harvest			25	21	19		11	8	4	1/28	25	

The cultivation of the vegetable is explained in the Calendar on the highlighted date.

*Ideal soil temperature for good germination.

Year-round cabbages

- Sow and plant in the greenhouse, under cover or in the open depending on the season and the climate of your garden
- Sow with the ascendant Moon in Pisces ♓
- Plant, hoe and earth up with the descending Moon in Cancer ♋ or Scorpio ♏

	Jan	Feb	Mar	Apr	May	Jun	Jul	Aug	Sep	Oct	Nov	Dec
Brussels sprouts												
Prepare and enrich soil		8/17	6/15	3/11/30						11/19	7/16	
Sow in nursery			25	21	19							
Transplant in nursery, maintain				3/11/30	9/27	5/24						
Plant, maintain				3/11/30	9/27	5/24	3/21/30	17/26	14/22	11/19		
Harvest	2/29	1/26	25						4	1/28	25	22
Chinese cabbage												
Prepare and enrich soil				3/11/30	9/27	5/24						
Sow in plot						14	11	8	4			
Thin, maintain							3/21/30	17/26	14/22	11/19	7/16	
Harvest									4	1/28	25	22
Head cabbage												
Prepare and enrich soil		8/17	6/15	3/11/30	19			8		11/19	7/16	
Sow in warm conditions	2/29	1/26	25	21					4			
Transplant in nursery		8/17	6/15	3/11/30	9/27	5/24		26	14/22	11/19		
Plant, maintain			6/15	3/11/30	9/27	5/24	3/21/30	17/26	14/22	11/19	7/16	
Harvest					19	14	11	8	4	1/28	25	22
Kale												
Prepare and enrich soil		8/17	6/15	3/11/30						11/19	7/16	
Sow in nursery				21	19	14						
Transplant in nursery, maintain					9/27	5/24	3/21/30					
Plant, maintain					9/27	5/24	3/21/30	17/26	14/22	11/19	7/16	
Harvest	2/29	1/26	25							1/28	25	22
Savoy cabbage												
Prepare and enrich soil		8/17	6/15	3/11/30						11/19	7/16	
Sow in nursery					19	14						
Transplant in nursery, maintain						5/24	3/21/30					
Plant, maintain						5/24	3/21/30	17/26	14/22	11/19	7/16	
Harvest	2/29	1/26	25						4	1/28	25	22

The cultivation of the vegetable is explained in the Calendar on the highlighted date.

Year-round salad leaves

- Sow and plant in the greenhouse, under cover or in the open depending on the season and the climate of your garden
- Sow with the ascending Moon in Pisces ♓
- Plant, hoe and earth up with the descending Moon in Cancer ♋ or Scorpio ♏

	Jan	Feb	Mar	Apr	May	Jun	Jul	Aug	Sep	Oct	Nov	Dec
Cress												
Sow	2/29	1/26	25	21	19	14	11	8	4	1/28	25	22
Sow			25	21	19	14						
Dandelion												
Sow		1/26	25	21	19	14						
Pull out, plant				3/11/30	9/27	5/24	3/21/30	17/26				
Endive (chicory)												
Curly endive												
Sow			25	21	19	14	11					
Transplant, plant, maintain				3/11/30	9/27	5/24	3/21/30	17/26	14/22	11/19	7/16	
Escarole												
Sow			25	21	19	14	11					
Transplant, plant, maintain				3/11/30	9/27	5/24	3/21/30	17/26	14/22	11/19	7/16	
Radicchio												
Sow					19	14						
Thin out, maintain						5/24	3/21/30	17/26	14/22	11/19		
Wild chicory												
Sow					19	14						
Thin out, maintain						5/24	3/21/30	17/26	14/22	11/19		
Lettuce												
Batavia												
Sow	2/29	1/26	25	21	19	14	11	8	4			
Transplant, plant, maintain		8/17	6/15	3/11/30	9/27	5/24	3/21/30	17/26	14/22	11/19	7/16	
'Cut and come again' lettuce												
Sow	2/29	1/26	25	21	19	14	11	8	4			
Transplant, plant, maintain		8/17	6/15	3/11/30	9/27	5/24	3/21/30	17/26	14/22	11/19	7/16	
Head lettuce												
Sow	2/29	1/26	25	21	19	14	11	8	4			
Transplant, plant, maintain	12/20	8/17	6/15	3/11/30	9/27	5/24	3/21/30	17/26	14/22			
Lamb's lettuce (mâche)												
Sow							11	8	4	1		
Romaine												
Sow		1/26	25	21	19	14	11	8				
Transplant, plant, maintain			6/15	3/11/30	9/27	5/24	3/21/30	17/26	14/22			
Winter lettuce												
Sow								8	4	1		
Transplant, plant, maintain	12/20	8/17	6/15	3/11/30	9/27				14/22	11/19	17/16	5/13
Purslane												
Sow	2/29	1/26	25	21	19	14	11	8				22
Rocket (arugula)												
Sow		1/26	25	21	19	14	11	8	4			

The cultivation of the vegetable is explained in the Calendar on the highlighted date.

Aromatic herbs

- Sow and plant in the greenhouse, under cover or in the open depending on the season and the climate of your garden
- Sow with the ascending Moon in Pisces ♓
- Plant, divide and prune with the descending Moon in Cancer ♋ or Scorpio ♏

		Jan	Feb	Mar	Apr	May	Jun	Jul	Aug	Sep	Oct	Nov	Dec
Annuals													
Basil	Sow in sheltered location			25	21								
	Plant				3/11/30	9/27							
Chervil	Sow in sheltered location	2/29	1/26									1/28	
	Sow in the sun			25	21					4			
	Sow in the shade					19	14	11	8				
	Thin, remove flowers		8/17	6/15	3/11/30	9/27	5/24	3/21/30	17/26	14/22	11/19	7/16	
Coriander (cilantro)	Sow				21	19	14			4			
Dill	Sow lightly				21	19	14						
Marjoram	Sow			25	21	19				4			
Parsley	Sow		1/26	25	21	19	14	11	8	4			
	Thin, remove flowers			6/15	3/11/30	9/27	5/24	3/21/30	17/26	14/22			
Perrenials													
Bay (laurel)	Plant, prune			6/15	3/11/30	9/27				14/22	11/19		
	Take cuttings								17/26	14/22			
Chive	Sow			25	21								
	Thin, transplant				3/11/30	9/27							
	Plant, divide			6/15	3/11/30	9/27				14/22	11/19		
Lemon-balm	Sow					19	14						
	Plant, divide			6/15	3/11/30	9/27				14/22	11/19		
Mint	Plant, divide			6/15	3/11/30	9/27							
	Cut back						5/24	3/21/30			11/19	7/16	
Oregano	Sow			25	21	19				4			
	Plant, divide			6/15	3/11/30	9/27				14/22	11/19		
Rosemary	Plant			6/15	3/11/30	9/27							
	Take cuttings				3/11/30	9/27			17/26	14/22			
Sage	Plant, prune			6/15	3/11/30	9/27							
	Take cuttings								17/26	14/22			
Savory	Plant			6/15	3/11/30	9/27				14/22			
	Take cuttings								17/26	14/22			
Sorrel	Sow		1/26	25	21	19	14						
	Plant, divide		8/17	6/15	3/11/30						11/19	7/16	
Tarragon	Plant, divide			6/15	3/11/30	9/27							
	Cut back, protect										11/19	7/16	
Thyme	Sow				21	19							
	Plant, divide				3/11/30	9/27				14/22	11/19		
	Prune						5/24	3/21/30	17/26				

The cultivation of the vegetable is explained in the Calendar on the highlighted date.

Root vegetables

- Sow and plant in the greenhouse, under cover or in the open depending on the season and the climate of your garden
- Sow with the ascendant Moon in Taurus ♉ or Capricorn ♑
- Do all other garden work with the descending Moon in Virgo ♍

Crop	Activity	Jan	Feb	Mar	Apr	May	Jun	Jul	Aug	Sep	Oct	Nov	Dec
t(root)	→ Sow (soil at 10 °C/50 °F*)			2/19/29	16/25	13/22	9/19						
	→ Thin, hoe				8	4/31	1/28	26	22	19	15		
	→ Harvest							26	22	19	15	11	
rrot	→ Sow (soil at 10 °C/50 °F*)	7/25	3/21	2/19/29	16/25	13/22	9/19	7/16	3/12/30	9/26	6/24	2/20/29	1/17/27
	→ Weed, thin	15	12	11	8	4/31	1/28	26	22	19	15	11	9
	→ Harvest				8	4/31	1/28	26	22	19	15	11	9
eriac	→ Sow (soil at 12 °C/53 °F*)		3/21	2/19/29	16/25	13/22							
	→ Transplant twice, plant			11	8	4/31	1/28						
	→ Harvest								22	19	15	11	
ory loof/ ve)	→ Sow (soil at 14 °C/57 °F*)					13/22	9/19						
	→ Thin, weed					31	1/28	26	22	19	15		
	→ Pull out, then replant**										15		
inese ichoke	→ Plant			11	8								
	→ Hoe, weed				8	4/31	1/28	26	22	19	15		
	→ Harvest	15	12	11							15	11	9
rlic	→ Plant, hoe	15	12	11							15	11	9
	→ Harvest					4/31	1/28	26	22				
ek	→ Sow (soil at 10 °C/50 °F*)	7/25	3/21	2/19/29	16/25	13/22			30	9/26			
	→ Thin, plant, hoe		12	11	8	4/31	1/28	26		19	15	11	9
	→ Harvest	15	12	11	8	4/31	1/28	26	22	19	15	11	9
ion loured)	→ Sow (soil at 10 °C/50 °F*)		3/21	2/19/29	16/25				12/30				
	→ Thin, plant, hoe				8	4/31	1/28	26		19	15	11	
	→ Harvest						1/28	26	22				
ion hite)	→ Sow (soil at 10 °C/50 °F*)	7/25	3/21	2/19/29	16/25				12/30				
	→ Thin, plant, hoe			11	8	4/31	1/28			19	15	11	
	→ Harvest					4/31	1/28						
tato	→ Plant		12	11	8								
	→ Earth up, hoe, harvest			11	8	4/31	1/28	26	22				
dish	→ Sow (soil at 12 °C/53 °F*)	7/25	3/21	2/19/29	16/25	13/22	9/19	7/16	3/12/30	9/26	6/24	2/20/29	1/17/27
	→ Thin, harvest	15	12	11	8	4/31	1/19/28	26	22	19	15	11	9
sify	→ Sow (soil at 15 °C/59 °F*)			2/19/29	16/25	13/22			3/12/30				
	→ Thin, hoe				8	4/31	1/28	26	22	19	15		
	→ Harvest	15	12								15	11	9
allot	→ Plant, weed	15	12	11	8	4/31	1/28	26			15	11	9
	→ Harvest						1/28	26	22				
nip	→ Sow (soil at 15 °C/59 °F*)	7/25	3/21	2/19/29	16/25	13/22	9/19	7/16	3/12/30				
	→ Thin, hoe, water		12	11	8	4/31	1/28	26	22	19	15		
	→ Harvest				8	4/31	1/28	26	22	19	15		

The cultivation of the vegetable is explained in the Calendar on the highlighted date.
*Ideal soil temperature for good germination.
** See more in leafy vegetables (p. 107).

Fruit vegetables

- Sow and plant in the greenhouse, under cover or in the open depending on the season and the climate of your garden
- Sow with the ascendant Moon in Aries ♈ or Sagittarius ♐
- Do all other work with the descending Moon in Leo ♌

	Jan	Feb	Mar	Apr	May	Jun	Jul	Aug	Sep	Oct	Nov	Dec
Aubergine												
→ Sow (in warm location at 20 °C/68 °F*)		2/20/29	18/28									
→ Transplant, plant, prune			8	4	2/29	25	22	19	15			
→ Harvest							5/15	2/11/29	7/25	4/22		
Beans												
→ Sow (soil at 10–12 °C/ 50–53 °F*)				24	11/21	8/17	5/15					
→ Hoe, earth up						25	22	19	15			
→ Harvest							5/15	2/11/29	7/25	4/22		
Broad beans (fava)												
→ Sow (soil at 8–10 °C/ 46–50 °F*)	6/23	2/20/29	18/28							4/22/31	1/19/28	16/25
→ Hoe, earth up, cut tops	13	9	8	4	2/29	25	22				9	6
→ Harvest				14/24	11/21	8/17	5/15	2/11/29				
Cucumber												
→ Sow (soil at 18 °C/64 °F*)			18/28	14/24	11/21	8/17						
→ Thin, plant, prune				4	2/29	25	22	19	15			
→ Harvest						8/17	5/15	2/11/29	7/25	4/22		
Marrow and courgette (zucchini)												
→ Sow (soil at 14 °C/ 57 °F*)			18/28	14/24	11/21	8/17	5/15					
→ Thin, plant, prune				4	2/29	25	22	19	15			
→ Harvest						8/17	5/15	2/11/29	7/25	4/22/31		
Melon												
→ Sow (soil at 20 °C/ 68 °F*)			18/28	14/24	11/21							
→ Transplant, plant, cut back				4	2/29	25	22	19				
→ Harvest							5/15	2/11/29	7			
Peas												
→ Sow (soil at 10 °C/ 50 °F*)	6/23	2/20/29	18/28	14/24	11/21				25	4/22/31	1/19/28	16/25
→ Hoe, earth up	13	9	8	4	2/29	25	22				9	6
→ Harvest				14/24	11/21	8/17	5/15					
Pepper (chilli and sweet)												
→ Sow (in warm location at 20 °C/68 °F*)		2/20/29	18/28									
→ Transplant, plant, cut back			8	4	2/29	25	22	19	15			
→ Harvest							5/15	2/11/29	7/25	4/22		
Strawberry												
→ Plant			8	4				19	15	13		
→ Harvest					11/21	8/17	5/15	2/11/29	7/25	4/22		
Tomato												
→ Sow (soil at 16–20 °C/ 60–68 °F*)		2/20/29	18/28									
→ Transplant, plant, prune			8	4	2/29	25	22	19	15			
→ Harvest						8/17	5/15	2/11/29	7/25	4/22		

The cultivation of the vegetable is explained in the Calendar on the highlighted date.

*Ideal soil temperature for good germination.

In the Orchard

- Plant, prune, clear and make cuttings with the descending Moon in Leo ♌
- Graft in the ascending Moon in Aries ♈ or Sagittarius ♐

		Jan	Feb	Mar	Apr	May	Jun	Jul	Aug	Sep	Oct	Nov	Dec
Fruit Trees and Shrubs													
Plant	→ Prepare planting holes, fertilise	13	9	8	4				19	15	13	9	6
	→ Plant fruit trees and soft-fruit shrubs	13	9	8	4					15	13	9	6
Prune	→ Crops with pips: apple, pear trees and grapes	13	9	8								9	6
	→ Apricot and peach trees		9	8									
	→ Soft-fruit bushes			9	8			22	19				
	→ When green, prune apples, pears, grapes						25	22	19				
	→ After the harvest, prune apricot and peach trees								19	15			
Treat trees	→ With white oil in winter	13	9									9	6
	→ With fungicide twice a year: before budding and when leaves fall		9	8							13	9	
Thin	→ Apples, pears, peaches					2/29	25						
Propagate	→ Make cuttings of soft-fruit shrubs		9	8								9	6
	→ Graft fruit-bearing trees			18/28	14/24			8/17	5/15	2/11/29			
	→ Layer grapes and kiwi			8	4	2/29	25						
Olive Trees													
	→ Plant			8									
	→ Prune, treat		9	8							13	9	
	→ Fertilise				4	2/29		22			13		

Wood for Timber and Heating

	Jan	Feb	Mar	Apr	May	Jun	Jul	Aug	Sep	Oct	Nov	Dec
Cut down large trees, cut up trunks, split logs	In descending Moon: January 11–22, February 7–18, March 5–16.									In descending Moon: October 10–21, November 6–17, December 3–15.		

The cultivation of the vegetable is explained in the Calendar on the highlighted date.

In the Ornamental Garden

- Thin, transplant, cut back, make cuttings, layer, divide and fertilise with the descending Moon in Gemini ♊ or Libra ♎
- Sow and graft with the ascending Moon in Aquarius ♒

Plant	Activity	Jan	Feb	Mar	Apr	May	Jun	Jul	Aug	Sep	Oct	Nov	Dec
Annual flowers													
nasturtium, petunia, zinnia, clarkia...	Sow	1/27	23	21	18	15	11			1/29			19
	Thin, transplant, plant	18	7/15	5/13	2/10/29	7/26	4/22/30	1/20/28			10/18		
Biennial flowers													
wallflower, forget-me-not, daisy, pansy...	Sow						11	9	5				
	Thin, transplant, plant							1/20/28	16/24	12/20	10/18		
Perennial flowers													
oriental poppy, hollyhock, columbine, aster, peony...	Sow			21		15	11	9	5	1/29	26	22	
	Thin, transplant, plant				2/10/29		4/22/30	1/20/28	16/24	12/20	10/18	6	
	Divide			5/13	2/10/29			28	16/24	12/20	10/18		
Perennial bulbs													
Spring flowering													
snowdrop, crocus, anemone, narcissus, hyacinth, tulip...	Plant		7/15	5/13						12/20	10/18	6/15	
	Divide		7/15	5/13		7/26	4/22/30						
Summer flowering													
madonna lily	Plant								16/24				
other lilies	Plant		7/15	5/13						20	10/18	6/15	
canna, dahlia, gladiola...	Plant	18	7/15	5/13	2/10/29	7/26							
	Thin					7/26	4/22/30	1/20/28	16/24	12/20			
	Pull out										10/18	6/15	
Perennial rhizomes													
iris	Plant, divide						4/22/30	1/20/28	16/24				
Perennial climbers													
clematis, honeysuckle, wisteria...	Plant	18	7/15	5/13	2/10/29					12/20	10/18	6/15	3/12/30
	Prune		7/15	5/13									
	Layer				2/10/29	7/26	4/22/30	1/20/28	16/24				
Roses													
	Plant	18	7/15	5/13								6/15	3/12/30
	Prune suckers		7/15	5/13							6/15		
	Remove dead leaves							1/20/28	16/24				
	Deadhead flowers					26	4/22/30	1/20/28	16/24	12/20	10/18		
	Take cuttings								16/24	12/20			
	Fertilise		7/15	5/13								6/15	3/12/30
	T-bud (shield graft)							9	5	1/29			
Spring or summer-blooming shrubs													
magnolia, forsythia, lilac, rhododendron, hydrangea...	Plant	18	7/15	5/13	2/10/29					12/20	10/18	6/15	3/12/30
	Prune			5/13	2/10/29		7/26	4/22/30			10/18		
	Take cuttings			5/13	2/10/29		7/26	4/22/30	1/20/28	16/24	12/20		
	Fertilise		7/15	5/13								6/15	3/12/30
	Graft		23	21			11	9	5	1/29			

The cultivation of the vegetable is explained in the Calendar on the highlighted date.

Trees, shrubs, leafy climbers and vines

- Plant, cut back, prune, cut stakes, clear and plant cuttings with the descending Moon in Cancer ♋ or Scorpio ♏.

		Jan	Feb	Mar	Apr	May	Jun	Jul	Aug	Sep	Oct	Nov	Dec
Conifers													
cedar, cypress, thuja, pine, fir, spruce…	Plant			6/15	3/11/30					14/22	11/19		
	Prune			6/15	3/11/30				17/26	14/22			
	Take cuttings								17/26	14/22			
Deciduous trees and shrubs													
birch, hornbeam, maple, beech, poplar, plane tree, prunus, willow…	Plant	12/20	8/17	6/15	3/11/30					14/22	11/19	7/16	5/13
	Prune		8/17	6/15	3/11/30		5/24	3/21/30	17/26	14/22			
	Thin	12/20	8/17									7/16	5/13
	Remove stakes	12/20	8/17									7/16	5/13
	Brush						5/24	3/21/30	17/26				
	Take cuttings		8/17	6/15			5/24	3/21/30	17/26	14/22	11/19	7/16	
Evergreen shrubs and bushes													
boxwood, spindle tree, holly, bay (laurel)…	Plant		8/17	6/15	3/11/30					14/22	11/19	7/16	
	Prune		8/17	6/15	3/11/30	9/27	5/24		17/26	14/22			
	Take cuttings		8/17	6/15					17/26	14/22			
Vines and climbers													
ivy, Virginia creeper…	Plant		8/17	6/15	3/11/30					14/22	11/19	7/16	5/13
	Prune			6/15		9/27	5/24	3/21/30	17/26				
	Take cuttings			6/15	3/11/30						11/19	7/16	

The lawn

- Sow with the ascending Moon in Pisces ♓
- Do all other tasks with the descending Moon in Cancer ♋ or Scorpio ♏.

		Jan	Feb	Mar	Apr	May	Jun	Jul	Aug	Sep	Oct	Nov	Dec
Bare spots	→ Rake the soil, spread mulch, roll			6/15	3/11/30	9/27			17/26	14/22			
	→ Sow, roll, water					21	19			4			
For new lawns	→ Prepare the soil		8/17	6/15	3/11/30			30	17/26	14/22			
	→ Spread compost		8/17	6/15	3/11/30				17/26	14/22			
	→ Level, rake, roll		8/17	6/15	3/11/30				17/26	14/22			
	→ Sow					21	19			4			
Yearly maintenance	→ Rake/scarify			6/15	3/11/30								
	→ Weed			6/15	3/11/30	9/27				14/22	11/19		
	→ Fertilise			6/15	3/11/30								5/13
	→ Mow, water			6/15	3/11/30	9/27	5/24	3/21/30	17/26	14/22	11/19		

In winter, don't walk on your lawn if it is frozen or under snow as you will damage the grass.

The cultivation of the vegetable is explained in the Calendar on the highlighted date.

Index

More books you might enjoy

Explore the natural world

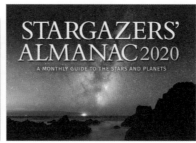

Enjoy nature with children

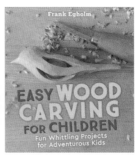

A glass of wine?

Have you tried our new Biodynamic Gardening Calendar app?

Based on the Maria Thun Biodynamic Calendar, the Biodynamic Gardening Calendar app is a quick, easy way to look up daily sowing and planting information, plus these great features:

- Automatically adjusts to your time-zone
- Filter activities by the crops you're growing
- Plan ahead by day, week or month

Try it for free!